YORK NOTES

PRIDE AND PREJUDICE

JANE AUSTEN

NOTES BY PAUL PASCOE
REVISED BY JULIA JONES

PEARSON

 YORK PRESS

YORK PRESS
322 Old Brompton Road, London SW5 9JH

PEARSON EDUCATION LIMITED
Edinburgh Gate, Harlow,
Essex CM20 2JE, United Kingdom
Associated companies, branches and representatives throughout the world

First published 1998
New editions 2002, 2010
This new and fully revised edition 2015

10 9 8 7 6 5 4 3 2

ISBN 978–1–4479–8222–7

Illustrated by Iris Compiet, and Alan Batley (page 70 only)

Phototypeset by Swales and Willis Ltd

Printed in China by Golden Cup

Photo credits: Graham Taylor/Shutterstock for page 8 bottom/Jane McIlroy/
Shutterstock for page 9 top/corund/Shutterstock for page 10 bottom/
rolleiflextlr/Thinkstock for page 12 bottom/yurchak/Shutterstock for page
13 bottom/John Gomez/Shutterstock for page 15 top/Ljupco/Thinkstock for
page 16 bottom/Richard Mann/Shutterstock for page 17 top/
demetriomancini/Thinkstock for page 18 bottom/© iStock/© petek arici for
page 19 middle/1000 Words/Shutterstock for page 20 bottom/© Lebrecht
Authors/Lebrecht Music & Arts/Corbis for page 23 middle/© iStock/© wragg
for page 24 bottom/BrAt82/Shutterstock for page 25 middle/BMJ/
Shutterstock for page 27 middle/AnjelikaGr/Shutterstock for page 28
bottom/© iStock/©Synergee for page 29 bottom/Swettlana Gordacheva/
Shutterstock for page 30 bottom/Adisa/Shutterstock for page 31 bottom/M.
Unal Ozmen/Shutterstock for page 33 top/Steve Buckley/Shutterstock for
page 35 top/david muscroft/Shutterstock for page 37 top/Andrii Muzyka/
Shutterstock for page 38 middle/Leemage/Getty Images for page 39
bottom/Neveshkin Nikolay/Shutterstock for page 42 middle/happydancing/
Shutterstock for page 43 middle/northwoodsphoto/Thinkstock for page 44
middle/jdm.foto/Shutterstock for page 46 top/© iStock/© LdF for page 48
middle/Ivan Montero Martinez/Shutterstock for page 52 bottom/© iStock/©
Vershinin-M for page 55 bottom/Galushko Sergey/Shutterstock for page 65
bottom/cynoclub/Shutterstock for page 66 bottom/Claudio Divizia/
Shutterstock for page 68 bottom/bunsview/Shutterstock for page 69 top/
Elena Kharichkina/Shutterstock for page 72 middle/Voyagerix/Shutterstock
for page 73 bottom/wavebreakmedia/Shutterstock for page 87 bottom

CONTENTS

PART FOUR:
THEMES, CONTEXTS AND SETTINGS

PART FIVE:
FORM, STRUCTURE AND LANGUAGE

PART SIX:
PROGRESS BOOSTER ★

PART SEVEN:
FURTHER STUDY AND ANSWERS

PREPARING FOR ASSESSMENT

HOW WILL I BE ASSESSED ON MY WORK ON *PRIDE AND PREJUDICE?*

All exam boards are different but whichever course you are following, your work will be examined through these four Assessment Objectives:

Assessment Objectives	Wording	Worth thinking about . . .
AO1	Read, understand and respond to texts. Students should be able to: ● maintain a critical style and develop an informed personal response ● use textual references, including quotations, to support and illustrate interpretations.	● How well do I know what happens, what people say, do, etc.? ● What do I think about the key ideas in the novel? ● How can I support my viewpoint in a really convincing way? ● What are the best quotations to use and when should I use them?
AO2	Analyse the language, form and structure used by a writer to create meanings and effects, using relevant subject terminology where appropriate.	● What specific things does the writer 'do'? What choices has Austen made? (Why this particular word, phrase or paragraph here? Why does this event happen at this point?) ● What effects do these choices create? (Suspense? Ironic laughter? Reflective mood?)
AO3	Show understanding of the relationships between texts and the contexts in which they were written.	● What can I learn about society from the book? (What does it tell me about wealth and inheritance in Austen's day, for example?) ● What was society like in Austen's time? Can I see it reflected in the story?
AO4	Use a range of vocabulary and sentence structures for clarity, purpose and effect, with accurate spelling and punctuation.	● How accurately and clearly do I write? ● Are there small errors of grammar, spelling and punctuation I can get rid of?

Look out for the Assessment Objective labels throughout your York Notes Study Guide – these will help to focus your study and revision!

The text used in this Study Guide is the Heinemann New Windmill Classics edition, 1994.

HOW TO USE YOUR YORK NOTES STUDY GUIDE

You are probably wondering what is the best and most efficient way to use your York Notes Study Guide on *Pride and Prejudice*. Here are three possibilities:

A **step-by-step** study and revision guide	A **'dip-in'** support when you need it	A **revision guide** after you have finished the novel
Step 1: Read Part Two as you read the novel as a companion to help you study it. **Step 2:** When you need to, turn to Parts Three to Five to focus your learning. **Step 3**: Then, when you have finished use Parts Six and Seven to hone your exam skills, revise and practise for the exam.	Perhaps you know the book quite well, but you want to check your understanding and practise your exam skills? Just look for the section which you think you need most help with and go for it!	You might want to use the Notes after you have finished your study, using Parts Two to Five to check over what you have learned, and then work through Parts Six and Seven in the immediate weeks leading up to your exam.

HOW WILL THE GUIDE HELP YOU STUDY AND REVISE?

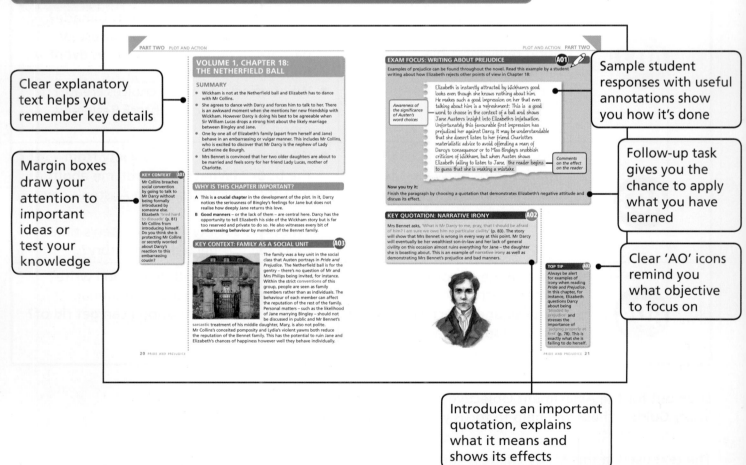

Clear explanatory text helps you remember key details

Margin boxes draw your attention to important ideas or test your knowledge

Sample student responses with useful annotations show you how it's done

Follow-up task gives you the chance to apply what you have learned

Clear 'AO' icons remind you what objective to focus on

Introduces an important quotation, explains what it means and shows its effects

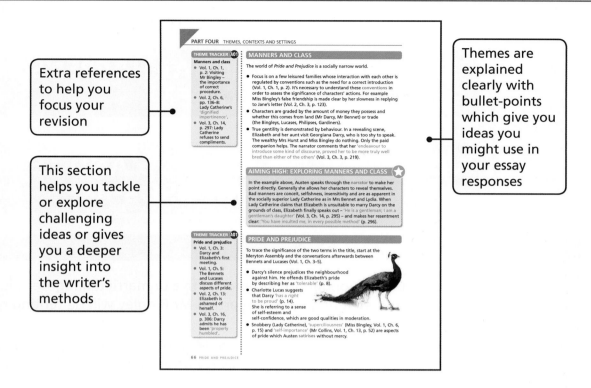

Extra references to help you focus your revision

This section helps you tackle or explore challenging ideas or gives you a deeper insight into the writer's methods

Themes are explained clearly with bullet-points which give you ideas you might use in your essay responses

Parts Two to Five each end with a **Progress and Revision Check:**

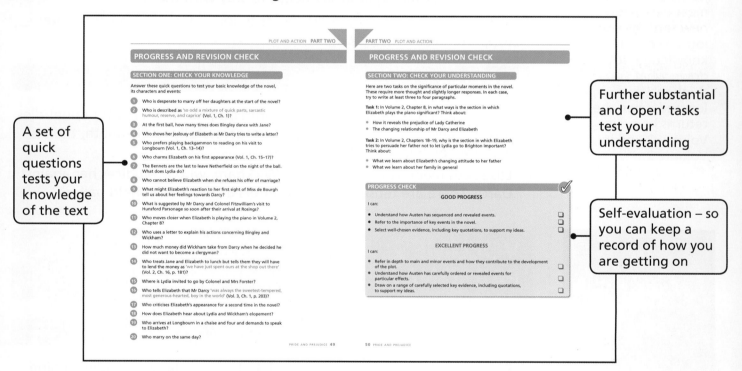

A set of quick questions tests your knowledge of the text

Further substantial and 'open' tasks test your understanding

Self-evaluation – so you can keep a record of how you are getting on

Don't forget Parts Six and Seven, with advice and practice on **improving your writing skills**:

- Focus on **difficult areas** such as **'context'** and **'inferences'**
- **Short snippets** of **other students' work** to show you how it's done (or not done!)
- Three, annotated **sample responses** to a task **at different levels**, with **expert comments**, to help you judge your own level
- **Practice questions**
- **Answers** to the **Progress and Revision Checks** and **Checkpoint** margin boxes

Now it's up to you! Don't forget – there's even more help on our website with more sample answers, essay planners and even online tutorials. Go to www.yorknotes.com to find out more.

PLOT SUMMARY: WHAT HAPPENS IN *PRIDE AND PREJUDICE*?

VOLUME 1: THE BENNETS AND THEIR NEIGHBOURS, HERTFORDSHIRE

CHAPTERS 1–12

- Mrs Bennet of Longbourn, mother of five unmarried daughters, is delighted that young, rich, unmarried Mr Bingley will be renting nearby Netherfield Park.
- Social visits are made and returned. Mr Bingley is attracted to beautiful Jane Bennet. His wealthy friend Darcy offends her sister Elizabeth before noticing her 'fine eyes' (Ch. 6, p. 21).
- Bingley's sisters invite Jane to Netherfield. Her mother's scheming results in her falling ill so she needs to stay with them.
- Elizabeth tramps across muddy fields to join her sister. This forces her to spend time with Darcy.

CHAPTERS 13–23

- Clergyman Mr Collins, who will inherit Longbourn when Mr Bennet dies, invites himself to stay. He proposes unsuccessfully to Elizabeth, then is accepted by her friend Charlotte Lucas.
- Elizabeth meets good-looking Mr Wickham, who prejudices her against Darcy. There are tense social encounters at the Netherfield ball.

VOLUME 2: A VISIT TO KENT, HUNSFORD PARSONAGE AND ROSINGS PARK

CHAPTERS 1–19

- Bingley and party move hastily back to London. Jane struggles to hide her misery. After Christmas she too goes to London, to stay with Mr and Mrs Gardiner (her aunt and uncle), but is ignored and then snubbed by Miss Bingley.
- In March Elizabeth goes to stay with Charlotte and Mr Collins at Hunsford Parsonage. She meets Darcy's snobbish aunt, Lady Catherine de Bourgh of Rosings Park.
- Darcy and his cousin Colonel Fitzwilliam arrive. Fitzwilliam reveals to Elizabeth that it was Darcy who forced Bingley to leave Jane.
- Darcy proposes to Elizabeth. She rejects him furiously.
- Darcy writes a letter to explain his actions. He tells her the truth about Wickham.

- Elizabeth returns home. Wickham and the regiment leave the area for Brighton. Mr Bennet allows his youngest daughter, Lydia, to go too. Elizabeth disagrees.

VOLUME 3: TO PEMBERLEY AND HOME AGAIN

CHAPTERS 1–3

- Elizabeth and the Gardiners go on a summer trip to Derbyshire. They are admiring Mr Darcy's house, Pemberley, when he appears, unexpectedly.
- Darcy is warmly welcoming. He introduces Elizabeth to his sister and invites Mr Gardiner fishing.

CHAPTERS 4–13

- Elizabeth receives letters from Jane: Lydia and Wickham have eloped. Darcy is shocked and sympathetic.
- Elizabeth realises how her feelings towards him have changed but assumes their relationship is over. She and the Gardiners hurry home to deal with the crisis.
- Mr Gardiner writes from London announcing that Wickham has agreed to marry Lydia. It is obvious that he has been paid to do this. But by whom?
- Lydia and Wickham arrive at Longbourn after their wedding. Lydia lets slip that Mr Darcy was at the ceremony.
- Mrs Gardiner tells Elizabeth, privately, that it was Darcy who paid Wickham.
- Bingley returns to Netherfield. He and Darcy come to visit the Bennets. It is not long before Bingley proposes to Jane and she accepts him.

CHECKPOINT 1

Elizabeth travels from her home in Hertfordshire to two other counties. Which are they?

CHAPTERS 14–19

- Lady Catherine de Bourgh visits Longbourn and tries to force Elizabeth to promise that she will never marry Darcy. Elizabeth refuses to be bullied.
- Darcy and Elizabeth finally have a chance to talk privately. She thanks him for saving Lydia. He proposes to her again and she accepts.
- Mr Bennet is worried that Elizabeth is marrying without love or respect. She is able to reassure him.
- The weddings of Elizabeth to Darcy and Jane to Bingley take place on the same day. Elizabeth is glad when she can finally escape Longbourn to live in Pemberley and it is not long before Jane and Bingley decide to follow her to Derbyshire.

REVISION FOCUS: KNOW THE TIMELINE

- Get the three-volume structure, time scheme and changes of setting clear in your mind.
- Draw a timeline which pinpoints the different locations where characters meet and interact over the course of the novel. Use the plot summary below to help you.

VOLUME 1, CHAPTERS 1–2: LIFE AT LONGBOURN

SUMMARY

- Mrs Bennet and her neighbours have heard that young, rich, unmarried Mr Bingley will be renting Netherfield Park.
- She presses her husband to visit him for the sake of their five unmarried daughters.
- Mr Bennet infuriates his wife by pretending to show no interest in this eligible bachelor. In fact he is one of the first people to call.

KEY CONTEXT (A03)

Jane Austen sets *Pride and Prejudice* in a narrow social world of gentry families (upper class but not titled) whose main activity seems to be socialising with each other. It is a world very similar (though not identical) to the world in which she herself lived.

WHY ARE THESE CHAPTERS IMPORTANT?

A They establish the importance of **marriage** and **money** as central themes and suggest an element of social competitiveness.

B We are introduced to the **Bennet household** and the incompatible characters of Mr and Mrs Bennet.

C Mr Bingley is introduced and so are other **neighbours** such as the Lucases.

D **Stylistically** these first chapters offer a mix of ironic comment by the narrator and revealing dialogue within the family.

KEY THEME: MARRIAGE AND MONEY (A02)

'It is a truth universally acknowledged, that a single man in possession of a good fortune, must be in want of a wife' (p. 1). This first sentence introduces a central theme in the novel – the importance of marriage and its connection with money and property. Mr and Mrs Bennet have five daughters and Mrs Bennet's one concern in life is to see them married. It is her 'business' (p. 3). At this point in the novel Austen does not tell the reader that the girls and their mother will be homeless after their father's death if they do not gain their own 'establishments' (Vol. 1, Ch. 22, p. 102). As a narrator she is critical of Mrs Bennet and sympathises with Mr Bennet's sarcastic teasing. These chapters also establish the strict social conventions that govern this small world. Mrs Bennet's comments about Mrs Long reveal the potential competiveness and self-seeking beneath the surface of politeness.

KEY CHARACTERS: MR AND MRS BENNET (A01)

This novel about marriage opens with a marriage that is clearly not a happy one. Mr Bennet's teasing of Mrs Bennet could be read as affectionate in a different context but the narrator soon makes it clear that husband and wife are incompatible: 'the experience of three and twenty years had been insufficient to make his wife understand his character' (p. 3). The dialogue shows Mr Bennet using his cleverness to make a fool of her in front of their children. He shows his weary contempt when he leaves the room 'fatigued' by her 'raptures' (p. 5). The narrator describes him as 'so odd a mixture' (p. 3) but shows no sympathy at all for Mrs Bennet, who is condemned as 'a woman of mean understanding, little information, and uncertain temper' (p. 3).

TOP TIP: WRITING ABOUT STYLE (A02)

It is important that you can write about key aspects of Jane Austen's **style** evident in Chapters 1–2. Make sure you can explain the effects of the following key features:

- **Irony:** The first sentence contains powerful words and phrases such as 'truth', 'universally acknowledged' and 'must'. The force of these words is undercut by the acknowledgement of ignorance 'However little known' (p. 1).

- **Characteristic speech rhythms:** Mrs Bennet tends towards exclamations and assertions, while Mr Bennet usually seems to prefer calm statements: 'You mistake me, my dear. I have a high respect for your nerves' (p. 3).

- **Narrator's voice:** Used to describe and condemn – as in the contemptuous adjectives applied to Mrs Bennet: 'mean', 'little', 'uncertain' (p. 3).

TOP TIP (A01)

Notice how skilfully and quickly the existence of the neighbours (Mrs Long and the Lucases) and the importance of their opinions are established in the brief opening chapter. As the novel progresses the neighbourhood almost becomes an additional character itself.

VOLUME 1, CHAPTERS 3–5: FIRST IMPRESSIONS

SUMMARY

- Mr Bennet refuses to discuss Mr Bingley. Mrs Bennet and her daughters manage only a glimpse before they and other local families all meet at the Meryton Assembly (a ball).

- Mr Bingley brings his two sisters (Caroline and Louisa), his brother-in-law (Mr Hurst) and his rich friend Mr Darcy. Bingley enjoys the evening; the others are unimpressed. Elizabeth Bennet overhears Darcy refusing to dance with her though he describes her as 'tolerable' (p. 8).

- Bingley is obviously attracted to Jane and she admits privately that she feels the same.

- The younger Lucases and Bennets meet to discuss the ball and the character of 'proud' (p. 14) Mr Darcy.

WHY ARE THESE CHAPTERS IMPORTANT?

A We are not only introduced to more of the main characters (especially Bingley, Darcy and Charlotte Lucas) but also shown them meeting each other and forming their own **first impressions.**

B Darcy is the hero of the novel and is viewed from a variety of **perspectives** – neighbourhood opinion (in the Assembly Room), Elizabeth's hurt feelings, general conversation between friends and some facts from the narrator.

C We glimpse the special **closeness** between Jane and Elizabeth.

D The narrator provides information about the **amount of money** people have and where it comes from, also some insight into Bingley's **personality** and his **friendship with Darcy** which will help us understand his later actions.

KEY THEME: PRIDE AND PREJUDICE (A02)

A bad first impression may lead to prejudice. Elizabeth (the heroine) is clever enough to recognise this but does not necessarily act on it: 'I could easily forgive *his* pride if he had not mortified *mine*!' (p. 14) Her sister Jane, however, 'would wish not to be too hasty in censuring any one' (p. 10). The concept of pride is shown to be complex – it can refer to good self-esteem as well as to arrogance. Different characters have points of view appropriate to them, for example Charlotte focuses on Darcy's family position. Austen uses the social setting of the ball to show how changeable and how harsh public opinion can be: 'His character was decided. He was the proudest, most disagreeable man in the world' (p. 7). It also shows how women were forced to be passive and wait for men to judge their attractiveness.

VOLUME 1, CHAPTER 6: SECOND IMPRESSIONS?

SUMMARY

- Small-scale socialising continues with a formal visit from the Bingley sisters to the Bennet sisters and an evening of music and dancing at the Lucases' house.
- Elizabeth Bennet and Charlotte Lucas discuss Jane's relationship with Bingley.
- Darcy shocks Caroline Bingley by telling her that he admires Elizabeth's 'fine eyes' (p. 21).

WHY IS THIS CHAPTER IMPORTANT?

A The key **theme** of **marriage as an economic necessity** is discussed by Charlotte and Elizabeth from different **perspectives**.

B **Problems** between Jane and Bingley due to Jane's habit of **concealing** her feelings are foreshadowed.

C **Darcy's physical response** to Elizabeth is forcing him to reconsider his first impressions. She, however, is much slower to think again.

KEY LANGUAGE: IRONY

On the surface Charlotte and Elizabeth's discussion of Jane is a gossip between friends. Look closely at what Charlotte is saying, however. She uses words such as 'disadvantage', 'opportunity', 'fixing', 'secure' (p. 16) which reveal her hard-headed, strategic approach to getting married. It is an example of narrative irony when Elizabeth says 'You know [...] you would never act in this way yourself' (p. 17). In fact it is exactly how Charlotte acts later in the story. Elizabeth has to learn that even friends may not be what they seem.

AIMING HIGH: ANALYSING CHARACTERS' ACTIONS ⭐

Notice how Austen achieves most of her effects by her careful choice of words (diction), her use of dialogue and her narrator's comments. She also positions herself inside a character's head and uses words to convey their thoughts – here Mr Darcy is shown re-considering his opinion of Elizabeth (p. 17). In addition Austen uses body language when characters are not being rational. In this chapter Darcy is 'caught' by the 'easy playfulness' (p. 18) of Elizabeth's manners  and is drawn towards her, almost against his will. Such movements are often Austen's means of suggesting unconscious sexual attraction.

CHECKPOINT 2 **A01**

How does Mary Bennet successfully 'purchase praise and gratitude' (p. 19)?

VOLUME 1, CHAPTERS 7–9: COUNTRY LIFE IN WINTER

SUMMARY

- The Militia arrive in Meryton. Mrs Bennet's sister and brother-in-law, Mr and Mrs Philips, help Kitty and Lydia Bennet to get to know the officers. Mr Bennet is unimpressed.
- The Bingley sisters invite Jane to dine at Netherfield. Her mother makes her go on horseback so that she will be forced to stay if it rains.
- Jane falls ill and Elizabeth walks across fields to join her at Netherfield.
- The Bingley sisters are shocked by Elizabeth's muddy skirt. She remains at Netherfield to care for Jane and gets to know the family better.
- Mrs Bennet visits Netherfield. Kitty and Lydia beg Mr Bingley to give a ball.

KEY CONTEXT (A03)

Austen began *Pride and Prejudice* in 1796 and it was finally published in 1813. Britain was at war with France almost continuously from the start of the French revolution in 1789 until 1815. A recent history by Jenny Uglow estimates that at this time one in five families were affected by recruitment into the armed forces, and two of Austen's brothers were in the Navy. The Militia were part of Britain's defence against possible invasion.

WHY ARE THESE CHAPTERS IMPORTANT?

A The **arrival of the Militia** introduces a new element into the neighbourhood. Their presence brings fun, for the younger girls especially, but is also **unsettling**. Mr Bennet disapproves but does nothing.

B **Mrs Bennet** is shown to be **ruthless** in her schemes to get her daughters married. Her shallow character and stupidity are embarrassing and potentially dangerous.

C **Elizabeth** is forced to spend time with the **Bingley household**. She continues to arouse Darcy's interest and Caroline Bingley's jealousy.

KEY CONTEXT: COUNTRY LIFE

Austen once wrote that 'four or five families in a country village is the very thing to work on'. That was the world in which she herself lived. These chapters give some insight into the dullness of country life in winter (especially for women) and the practical difficulties of getting about. Families were forced together, particularly in the evenings, and this could put strain on relationships. The arrival of officers of the Militia would have had a strong impact on social life in a quiet country town.

TOP TIP A02

Characters often reveal themselves by their attitude to reading. Notice the exchange between Elizabeth, Mr Hurst, Caroline Bingley and her brother. What does it tell you about each person?

EXAM FOCUS: CHARACTERISTIC SPEECH A02

Always be alert to how Austen develops her characters through the way they speak and the words they choose. Read this example by a student of such an analysis:

> As soon as Elizabeth leaves the dinner table Caroline Bingley begins 'abusing her', criticising her manners and appearance. Caroline's timing is significant as it shows how calculating she is – her mask of politeness drops when Elizabeth is no longer in the room. Her sister, Louisa, joins in: 'I hope you saw her petticoat, six inches deep in mud.' This is a good example of Austen focusing on a specific detail to reveal the small-mindedness of these two conceited sisters. All four characters discuss Elizabeth's walk across the fields. They all have their own perspective on this single incident. Bingley focuses on Elizabeth's 'affection' for Jane – who is uppermost in his mind. Caroline tries to use the incident to prejudice Darcy against Elizabeth by assuming the effect Elizabeth's unladylike behaviour will have.

Comments on the significance of Caroline's timing

Shows awareness of Austen's use of concrete detail

Expands on the idea to include new references

Now you try it:

This paragraph needs a final sentence that discusses Darcy's answer and what it shows about him. Begin: *In fact, Darcy ....*

VOLUME 1, CHAPTER 10: ANOTHER EVENING AT NETHERFIELD

SUMMARY

- Darcy writes a letter to his sister.
- A discussion about letter writing almost becomes an argument.
- Darcy asks Elizabeth to dance but she again refuses.

WHY IS THIS CHAPTER IMPORTANT?

A More evidence is provided of **Caroline Bingley's pursuit of Darcy** and dislike of Elizabeth.

B The **contrasting** characters of Bingley and Darcy are explored further.

C **Darcy feels** 'bewitched' by Elizabeth but assumes he will not let the relationship develop any further because of 'the inferiority of her connections' (p. 42).

KEY CHARACTERS: CAROLINE BINGLEY

An author can develop main characters by showing them in relationship to others. Here Caroline Bingley, a minor character, interrupts Darcy with constant flattery as he tries to write a letter. We are implicitly invited to contrast this with Elizabeth's quickness of thought and independent spirit. Darcy is polite but also determined – we can see that he is a strong personality. In order to flatter him, Caroline is prepared to denigrate her own brother, criticising his 'careless' letter writing (p. 38). Bingley's response shows his gentle nature and Elizabeth is unexpectedly tactful as she tries to soothe possible hurt feelings.

AIMING HIGH: EXPLORING SIMPLE EVENTS

Austen introduces narrative moments that reveal a great deal about relationships, status and power. Consider how Darcy perceives the Bingley sisters' rudeness when they turn onto a path which is too narrow to allow Elizabeth to walk beside them. This simple event is both poignant and telling in terms of plot and character development.

KEY QUOTATION: DARCY IS BEWITCHED **A02**

Austen tells us that 'Darcy had never been so bewitched by any woman as he was by [Elizabeth]' (p. 42). 'Bewitched' may seem a slightly surprising choice of word for the rational, strong-minded Mr Darcy but is echoed much later when Lady Catherine accuses Elizabeth of using 'arts and allurements' (Vol. 3, Ch. 14, p. 293) to attract him. It is insulting, as it implies no one could fall in love with Elizabeth simply for what she is, but it also suggests Darcy is not as fully in control of his emotions as he likes to think.

KEY CONTEXT **A03**

Letter writing was a key method of communication in Jane Austen's time and she and her family exchanged hundreds of letters when they were apart. However it was restricted by people's ability not only to write but also to afford the postage – most poor people could not.

VOLUME 1, CHAPTERS 11–12: JANE'S RECOVERY

SUMMARY

- Jane is well enough to spend the evening downstairs being looked after by Bingley.
- Caroline tries to read a book.
- Elizabeth and Darcy have a quick-fire conversation which, once again, leaves Darcy worried about the extent of the attraction he feels for her.
- Finally Jane and Elizabeth return home to Longbourn. Their father is glad to see them. Their mother is not.

WHY ARE THESE CHAPTERS IMPORTANT?

A **Bingley's behaviour** makes it obvious that he really cares for Jane.

B In this portrait of a quiet country evening Jane Austen shows **how people define themselves** by what they do. For example, Mr Hurst goes to sleep and Mrs Hurst plays with her bracelets – thus revealing their empty minds.

C Elizabeth and Darcy show that they are **well-matched** by their quick, sparkling conversation. They are laughing and arguing at the same time.

KEY LANGUAGE: COMEDY (A02)

Pride and Prejudice can be considered as a comic novel. Sometimes it is the narrator's comment that underlines the gap between what a character says and what she or he does. An example of this is Caroline Bingley struggling to read the second volume of Darcy's chosen book. She is constantly stopping and interrupting. Finally 'she gave a great yawn and said, "[...] How much sooner one tires of anything than a book!" [...] She then yawned again, threw aside her book, and cast her eyes around the room in search of some amusement' (pp. 44–5). A sense of humour is part of Elizabeth's personality: 'Follies and nonsense, whims and inconsistencies *do* divert me, I own, and I laugh at them whenever I can' (p. 46). Her half-laughing argument with Darcy might lead the reader to guess that she is more attracted to him than she realises.

> **CHECKPOINT 3** (A01)
>
> Why do the Bingley sisters appear in good spirits at this time?

REVISION FOCUS: OBSERVING CHARACTER DEVELOPMENT

Austen sometimes enables her readers to see what is happening before a character is aware of it. List the pieces of evidence up to Chapter 12 which show that Darcy is attracted to Elizabeth. Can you find any that suggest she is attracted to him?

VOLUME 1, CHAPTERS 13–14: MR COLLINS INVITES HIMSELF TO LONGBOURN

SUMMARY

- Mr Bennet's cousin, Mr Collins, invites himself to stay.
- Mrs Bennet is initially hostile as Mr Collins will inherit Longbourn when Mr Bennet dies – thus potentially making her and her daughters homeless. However, his expressed wish to offer 'amends' (p. 51) helps her decide to make him welcome.
- Mr Collins's main topic of conversation is his patroness Lady Catherine de Bourgh. He is shocked when asked to read a novel.

TOP TIP (A02)

When Elizabeth asks, 'Can [Mr Collins] be a sensible man, sir?' after listening to the content of his letter, Mr Bennet accurately identifies his 'mixture of servility and self-importance' (p. 52). Letters are a key part of the structure of *Pride and Prejudice*. It is important to notice where they occur and what effect they have.

WHY ARE THESE CHAPTERS IMPORTANT?

A The **introduction of Mr Collins** – and his frequent references to Lady Catherine – begins a new storyline and has considerable significance for the overall plot.

B Mr Collins's **letter** of introduction is one of many examples where Austen allows a **character** to reveal more about themselves than they intend.

KEY CONTEXT: A PATRIARCHAL SOCIETY (A03)

Today it would be almost unthinkable for Mr Collins to be legally able to inherit the Longbourn estate and make Mrs Bennet and her daughters homeless just because he is male. Primogeniture (all property going to the oldest son) was usual in Jane Austen's time but Lady Catherine de Bourgh's family chose to be outside the male inheritance system – and she is hardly an admirable example. Male inheritance is the hard economic fact that makes it so important for the girls to find husbands. Mr Collins is right to say that his cousins' beauty will help them be 'well disposed of in marriage' (p. 53).

REVISION FOCUS: CHARACTERS AND THEIR REACTIONS

CHECKPOINT 4 (A01)

What do Mr Collins's words to Lydia and his pleasure at backgammon reveal of his true character?

Every member of the Bennet family reacts to this new arrival, Mr Collins, in an entirely characteristic way. Look at how each person responds to his letter and make a list. Describing characters' reactions is an aspect of character development and also evidence of Austen's comic viewpoint. *Pride and Prejudice* is full of humorous examples of people behaving predictably. Challenge yourself to spot some more.

VOLUME 1, CHAPTERS 15–17: ELIGIBLE BACHELORS?

SUMMARY

- Mr Collins reveals that he is looking for a wife. Jane is his first choice but when he is told that she is almost engaged to Bingley, he switches to Elizabeth. He has no real feelings for either.
- The Bennet sisters meet handsome Mr Wickham, who has just joined the regiment.
- Darcy and Bingley arrive and Elizabeth notices how shocked Darcy and Wickham are when they see each other.
- There is an informal social gathering at the home of Mrs Bennet's sister, Mrs Philips. This gives Elizabeth an opportunity to get to know Wickham. He wastes no time telling her how badly Darcy has behaved.
- Jane is unwilling to believe Wickham's story.
- The Bennets and Mr Collins are invited to a ball at Netherfield.

KEY QUOTATION A02

Elizabeth says of Wickham 'there was truth in his looks' (p. 71). In fact she has been misled by his superficial attractiveness into believing his story without any proof.

WHY ARE THESE CHAPTERS IMPORTANT?

A Mr Collins's matrimonial **intentions** become clear.

B Wickham makes an excellent **first impression** – he is good-looking and charming.

CHECKPOINT 5 A01

Why is Elizabeth so ready to believe Wickham's story? Does this suggest her judgement of people is poor, or that Wickham is especially persuasive?

AIMING HIGH: APPEARANCE AND REALITY A01

Thinking about the gap between appearance and reality can lead to a richer understanding of characters, events and style in *Pride and Prejudice*. Much later in the story Elizabeth contrasts Wickham and Darcy when she is talking to Jane: 'There was certainly some great mismanagement in the education of those two young men. One has got all the goodness, and the other all the appearance of it' (Vol. 2, Ch. 17, p. 186).

KEY CHARACTER: INTRODUCING MR WICKHAM A02

By introducing the two new characters Mr Collins and Mr Wickham so close together in the story, Austen would have expected readers to contrast the two men – just as Elizabeth and her sisters do. However, while the narrator makes it perfectly clear that Mr Collins is a pompous caricature, there is no guidance at all about Wickham. Compare this to the way that the other eligible bachelors, Bingley and Darcy, have been introduced. There has been detailed information about their incomes, families, personalities. About Wickham there is nothing.

VOLUME 1, CHAPTER 18: THE NETHERFIELD BALL

SUMMARY

- Wickham is not at the Netherfield ball and Elizabeth has to dance with Mr Collins.

- She agrees to dance with Darcy and forces him to talk to her. There is an awkward moment when she mentions her new friendship with Wickham. However Darcy is doing his best to be agreeable when Sir William Lucas drops a strong hint about the likely marriage between Bingley and Jane.

- One by one all of Elizabeth's family (apart from herself and Jane) behave in an embarrassing or vulgar manner. This includes Mr Collins, who is excited to discover that Mr Darcy is the nephew of Lady Catherine de Bourgh.

- Mrs Bennet is convinced that her two older daughters are about to be married and feels sorry for her friend Lady Lucas, mother of Charlotte.

KEY CONTEXT (A03)

Mr Collins breaches social convention by going to talk to Mr Darcy without being formally introduced by someone else. Elizabeth 'tried hard to dissuade' (p. 81) Mr Collins from introducing himself. Do you think she is protecting Mr Collins or secretly worried about Darcy's reaction to this embarrassing cousin?

WHY IS THIS CHAPTER IMPORTANT?

A This is **a crucial chapter** in the development of the plot. In it, Darcy notices the seriousness of Bingley's feelings for Jane but does not realise how deeply Jane returns this love.

B **Good manners** – or the lack of them – are central here. Darcy has the opportunity to tell Elizabeth his side of the Wickham story but is far too reserved and private to do so. He also witnesses every bit of **embarrassing behaviour** by members of the Bennet family.

KEY CONTEXT: FAMILY AS A SOCIAL UNIT (A03)

The family was a key unit in the social class that Austen portrays in *Pride and Prejudice*. The Netherfield ball is for the gentry – there's no question of Mr and Mrs Philips being invited, for instance. Within the strict conventions of this group, people are seen as family members rather than as individuals. The behaviour of each member can affect the reputation of the rest of the family. Personal matters – such as the likelihood of Jane marrying Bingley – should not be discussed in public and Mr Bennet's sarcastic treatment of his middle daughter, Mary, is also not polite.

Mr Collins's conceited pomposity and Lydia's violent yawns both reduce the reputation of the Bennet family. This has the potential to ruin Jane and Elizabeth's chances of happiness however well they behave individually.

EXAM FOCUS: WRITING ABOUT PREJUDICE (A01)

Examples of prejudice can be found throughout the novel. Read this example by a student writing about how Elizabeth rejects other points of view in Chapter 18:

> Elizabeth is instantly attracted by Wickham's good looks even though she knows nothing about him. He makes such a good impression on her that even talking about him is a 'refreshment'. This is a good word to choose in the context of a ball and shows Jane Austen's insight into Elizabeth's infatuation. Unfortunately this favourable first impression has prejudiced her against Darcy. It may be understandable that she doesn't listen to her friend Charlotte's materialistic advice to avoid offending a man of Darcy's 'consequence' or to Miss Bingley's snobbish criticism of Wickham, but when Austen shows Elizabeth failing to listen to Jane, the reader begins to guess that she is making a mistake.

Awareness of the significance of Austen's word choices

Comments on the effect on the reader

Now you try it:

Finish the paragraph by choosing a quotation that demonstrates Elizabeth's negative attitude and discuss its effect.

KEY QUOTATION: NARRATIVE IRONY (A02)

Mrs Bennet asks, 'What is Mr Darcy to me, pray, that I should be afraid of him? I am sure we owe him no particular civility' (p. 83). The story will show that Mrs Bennet is wrong in every way at this point. Mr Darcy will eventually be her wealthiest son-in-law and her lack of general civility on this occasion almost ruins everything for Jane – the daughter she is boasting about. This is an example of **narrative irony** as well as demonstrating Mrs Bennet's prejudice and bad manners.

TOP TIP (A02)

Always be alert for examples of irony when reading *Pride and Prejudice*. In this chapter, for instance, Elizabeth questions Darcy about being 'blinded by prejudice' and stresses the importance of 'judging properly at first' (p. 78). This is exactly what she is failing to do herself.

VOLUME 1, CHAPTERS 19–21: MR COLLINS PROPOSES

SUMMARY

- Mr Collins proposes to Elizabeth and finds it hard to accept her refusal.
- Mr and Mrs Bennet offer opposing points of view.
- Charlotte Lucas arrives in the midst of the crisis.
- Wickham tells Elizabeth that he avoided the Netherfield ball for tactful reasons. He walks her back to Longbourn and she introduces him to her parents.
- Caroline Bingley sends Jane a note to say they are leaving Netherfield for London and are unlikely to return.

WHY ARE THESE CHAPTERS IMPORTANT?

A Mr Collins's proposal and Elizabeth's rejection is a key scene for the understanding of both their **characters** and also the central **theme** of **marriage**. Should it be for love or for security?

B Issues of **gender** are also highlighted in Mr Collins's attitudes to women and in the Bennet sisters' inability to inherit their home.

C **Romantic matters** are becoming complicated. Elizabeth, so clear and decisive with Mr Collins, is growing more obviously attracted to Wickham. The Bingleys' departure from Netherfield is a serious blow for Jane's hopes.

KEY CONTEXT

Mr Collins's ridiculous ideas about the behaviour of 'young ladies' (p. 89) are comic, but there is also a feeling of threat in Chapter 19, expressed through reminders of what will happen to Elizabeth and her sisters if they don't marry. We see how vulnerable they are, and that power commonly lies with men in this society.

KEY CHARACTERS: MR COLLINS AS CARICATURE

Austen presents Mr Collins as a **caricature** rather than as a rounded human being whose feelings might be hurt by Elizabeth's rejection: 'though his pride was hurt, he suffered in no other way' (p. 94). Although he presents himself as generous about money, the fact that he mentions it at all in a proposal of marriage is also revealing: 'it is by no means certain that another offer of marriage will ever be made you. Your portion is unhappily so small that it will in all likelihood undo the effects of your loveliness and amiable qualifications' (p. 91).

REVISION ACTIVITY: MR COLLINS'S EGOTISM

Work though Chapter 19 noting:

● How much Mr Collins says about himself
● How much he says about Lady Catherine
● How confident he is that he knows about women
● How little he listens to Elizabeth

KEY CONTEXT: ELIZABETH DEMANDS RESPECT

Austen would certainly have been aware of Mary Wollstonecraft's *A Vindication of the Rights of Woman*, published in 1792. We don't know exactly what Austen thought about women's rights but it is significant that Elizabeth, her **heroine**, demands to be taken seriously as a person, not dismissed or patronised because of her gender: 'Do not consider me now as an elegant female [...], but as a rational creature speaking the truth from her heart' (p. 91). You could contrast the **style** of  Mr Collins's long-winded sentences with Elizabeth's brief, forceful, unambiguous statements, such as 'Can I speak plainer?' (p. 91)

KEY QUOTATION: BALANCED SENTENCES

Mr Bennet is not a perfect father and his poor relationship with his wife is a weakness in the family. However he is rational, intelligent and humorous and on this occasion he deals with the situation decisively. 'Your mother will never see you again if you do *not* marry Mr Collins, and I will never see you again if you *do*' (p. 93). Austen expresses the balance and clarity of Mr Bennet's mind through the balance and clarity of this sentence. Elizabeth shares this quality of rational thought and clear expression. For example, she tells Mr Collins, 'You could not make *me* happy, and I am convinced that I am the last woman in the world who would make *you* so' (p. 90).

KEY CONTEXT A03

Do not underestimate the importance of this moment in the novel. If Elizabeth had accepted Mr Collins she could have saved her mother and sisters as well as herself from potential homelessness after her father's death. Mr Collins's warning that she may not receive another such offer is entirely plausible but she is prepared to sacrifice financial security for personal feeling and freedom. This is key to understanding her character and also to the author's views about true reasons for marriage.

TOP TIP A02

It's a good idea to collect a range of words to describe a character. Mr Collins is 'pompous' (Vol. 1, Ch. 15, p. 59) but he is many other things as well. See what other adjectives you can find.

VOLUME 1, CHAPTERS 22–3: MR COLLINS ACHIEVES HIS PURPOSE

SUMMARY

- Charlotte continues to listen patiently to Mr Collins. Elizabeth assumes this is out of simple kindness but Charlotte has an ulterior motive.
- Charlotte's plan succeeds. Mr Collins proposes to her and she accepts. The Lucas family are delighted.
- Charlotte and Elizabeth have a difficult conversation. Elizabeth feels she has lost her friend and is closer than ever to her sister Jane.
- Mrs Bennet makes everyone's lives miserable.

WHY ARE THESE CHAPTERS IMPORTANT?

A Elizabeth and Charlotte's conversation clarifies their opposing ideas on the theme of **marriage.**

B These chapters are also significant for the theme of **family.** Charlotte's family feel economic relief at her choice, while in the Bennet household the selfish complaints of Mrs Bennet dominate.

C The **structure** of the novel begins to shift to a new **storyline** which will move the **action** from Elizabeth's home neighbourhood to Kent.

CHECKPOINT 6

How is Mrs Bennet's reaction to the news of Charlotte's engagement typical of her character?

KEY THEME: VIEWS ON MARRIAGE

You can explore the theme of marriage via the different perspectives of each character. For example, Charlotte's acceptance of Mr Collins is based on her need for security. 'I am not romantic you know. I never was. I ask only a comfortable home' (p. 105). Elizabeth is more romantic: 'she could not have supposed it possible that [Charlotte] would have sacrificed every better feeling to worldly advantage' (p. 105). Mrs Bennet is full of recrimination and sees herself as the principal victim (p. 106). The Lucases are delighted and Lady Lucas even begins to wonder how soon Mr Bennet might die so her daughter will be mistress of Longbourn.

TOP TIP

These chapters mark a further step on Elizabeth's journey to a deeper understanding of other people. Previously she assumed that because she and Charlotte were friends they must share similar values. She had not looked beneath the surface, but here she realises that she and Charlotte have quite different ideas and motivations.

KEY CONTEXT: MARRIAGE AND FAMILY

Check the reaction of Charlotte's sisters and brothers. 'The younger girls formed hopes of *coming out* a year or two earlier than they might otherwise have done; and the boys were relieved of their apprehension of Charlotte's dying an old maid' (p. 102). In many families the younger girls were not allowed to attend dances and join adult society until the older ones were married. This was called 'coming out'. It was also expected that brothers would support their unmarried sisters (as Jane Austen's brothers did).

VOLUME 2, CHAPTERS 1–3: DISAPPOINTMENT FOR JANE

SUMMARY

- Caroline Bingley writes to tell Jane that they will be remaining in London. She drops hints about Bingley growing closer to Darcy's sister.

- Jane assumes this means that Bingley did not really care for her and struggles to continue to think well of everyone. Elizabeth guesses that his friends have interfered and is angry on Jane's behalf.

- Wickham becomes a frequent visitor to Longbourn.

- Mrs Bennet's brother, Mr Gardiner, comes to stay for Christmas with his wife and children.

- Mrs Gardiner is a good influence. She warns Elizabeth against Wickham and invites Jane to return to London with them to get away from her mother and Longbourn.

- Wickham turns his attention to Miss King, who has inherited a large sum of money.

WHY ARE THESE CHAPTERS IMPORTANT?

A The difference in **character** and **outlook** between Jane and Elizabeth is illustrated.

B **Letters** become increasingly important as a means of advancing the **plot** as well as illustrating character.

C The Gardiners provide **a positive perspective** on family life. They are an example of a good marriage and sensitive responsible parenting.

KEY QUOTATION: FREE INDIRECT SPEECH **A02**

Elizabeth shows good understanding of Bingley: 'much as she had always been disposed to like him, she could not think without anger, hardly without contempt, on that easiness of temper, that want of proper resolution which now made him the slave of his designing friends' (p. 111). This is an example of free indirect speech (reflecting on events from inside Elizabeth's head) and allows us to share her perception that Bingley's faults are closely linked to his virtues. We see her rationality in the balanced pattern of clauses but also her potential for emotion in the strong words 'anger' and 'contempt'.

CHECKPOINT 7 **A01**

Why is Mr Bennet's joke about Wickham jilting Elizabeth ironic?

VOLUME 2, CHAPTERS 4–5: TO HUNSFORD PARSONAGE

SUMMARY

- It is March. Elizabeth sets out to visit Charlotte in Kent together with Charlotte's father (Sir William) and sister (Maria). They spend a night at the Gardiners' home in London.
- Mrs Gardiner invites Elizabeth to join herself and her husband on a 'tour of pleasure' in the summer (p. 128).
- Mr and Mrs Collins welcome the visitors to their home, Hunsford Parsonage.
- Lady Catherine de Bourgh's daughter and her companion pass by and invite them to dine at Rosings Park.

WHY ARE THESE CHAPTERS IMPORTANT?

A The **change of location** brings a change of storyline and moves the **plot** forward.

B Insight into the Collins's home life expands the **theme** of **marriage** in order to gain a home and financial security.

CHECKPOINT 8 (A01)

Why is Mrs Gardiner's remembrance of Mr Darcy misleading?

KEY THEME: CLASS (A01)

The **theme** of class becomes more obvious as the novel progresses. The Gardiners are tradespeople. This allows Caroline Bingley to despise them automatically although her brother shows his good-heartedness by saying that this is nothing to do with Jane and Elizabeth. The Bingley sisters prefer to forget that their own fortune originally came from trade. Mr Darcy's money comes from land and so does Mr Bennet's. The Gardiners, however, represent honesty, good sense, good manners and true gentility. Mr Darcy recognises these qualities as soon as he finally meets them in person (Vol. 3, Ch. 1, p. 209).

KEY CHARACTER: ELIZABETH

Many of Jane Austen's **characters** are one-dimensional – they lack the ability to develop or surprise us. However, both Elizabeth and Darcy are prepared to learn from their mistakes, extend their self-knowledge, and think again. This is appropriate for a **hero** and **heroine.** Here Elizabeth shows her essential quality of fair-mindedness as she begins to repair her friendship with Charlotte. She is perceptive enough to notice many of Charlotte's survival strategies, such as encouraging Mr Collins to work in his garden to keep him out of the house, and she acknowledges that 'it was all done very well' (p. 131). Charlotte is strategically clever. She has married to gain 'a comfortable home' (Vol. 1, Ch. 22, p. 105) and now she is making the best of it.

KEY FORM: THE THREE-VOLUME NOVEL

The three-volume novel was standard in Austen's time as it suited the users of the circulating libraries. Note how Austen uses the form to develop the plot. Each volume has a new main location which allows characters to behave in slightly different ways. The changes have all been set up in advance: for example Mr Collins spoke about the grandeur of Rosings and Lady Catherine in the first volume (Ch. 16, p. 62) and already, in this second volume, there has been mention of the summer tour which will finally take Elizabeth to Pemberley.

AIMING HIGH: AUSTEN'S DICTION ⭐

When writing about Jane Austen's diction you are likely to mention her use of **abstract nouns** such as 'greatness' (p. 132). Writers today often keep their language concrete (specific) and avoid abstraction. This was not the case in Austen's time and usually her more refined characters use more

intellectual language. However, you might like to list the occasions when Austen uses a very brief, concrete word and what effect she gains by this technique. For example, when she sees Miss de Bourgh's carriage stop at the parsonage gate Maria Lucas insists that Elizabeth hurries downstairs 'for there is such a sight to be seen! I will not tell you what it is' (p. 132). When Elizabeth has seen the 'wonder', she comments 'I expected at least that the pigs were got into the garden; and here is nothing but Lady Catherine and her daughter!' The emphasis of the sentence falls on the word 'pigs'. Elizabeth is implicitly criticising the fuss Maria has made about two quite normal human visitors. It is disrespectful to hint that pigs would have been more interesting and suggests that Elizabeth will not be intimidated by grandeur.

> **CHECKPOINT 9** (A01)
>
> What does Elizabeth's reaction to the sight of Miss de Bourgh tell us of her feelings towards Darcy? Are they quite what they seem?

VOLUME 2, CHAPTERS 6–7: DINNER AT ROSINGS

SUMMARY

- Mr Collins prepares his guests for the grandeur of Rosings.
- They are introduced to Lady Catherine and her daughter.
- Lady Catherine asks Elizabeth a series of personal questions about herself and her family. Elizabeth resents this but does her best to remain polite.
- Sir William returns home and Elizabeth and Maria fit into the routine of life at the Parsonage and invitations to Rosings.
- Mr Darcy and his cousin Colonel Fitzwilliam arrive to stay at Rosings and are surprisingly quick to visit the Parsonage.

WHY ARE THESE CHAPTERS IMPORTANT?

A We are introduced to Lady Catherine de Bourgh, another caricature. She shows that **money** and high social **class** do not necessarily imply refinement or good manners. Her type of **pride** is snobbery and arrogance.

B Rosings Park is the key **setting** for Volume 2 – the Lucases are overwhelmed, Elizabeth is not – further evidence for her strong character and ability to think for herself.

CHECKPOINT 10 (A01)

What is suggested by the fact that Darcy and his cousin visit Hunsford so soon after their arrival at Rosings?

KEY CHARACTER: LADY CATHERINE DE BOURGH (A01)

We soon learn that, despite her title, Lady Catherine is every bit as impertinent (rude and nosy) as Mrs Bennet. In the world of *Pride and Prejudice* it is not good manners to ask too many personal questions of a new acquaintance and Elizabeth is irritated at being asked her age. Lady Catherine's evident surprise at her refusal to give a direct reply prompts Elizabeth to speculate that she may be the first person to stand up to her. '"Upon my word," said her ladyship, "you give your opinion very decidedly for so young a person"' (p. 138).

TOP TIP: WRITING ABOUT SERVANTS (A01)

It can sometimes help you extend your thinking if you consider what is not included in *Pride and Prejudice*. All writers and artists have to choose their special focus and this always means excluding other possibilities. Austen concentrates so narrowly on the leisured social class that working people are almost invisible. This does not mean that they are insignificant. At Rosings the servants are listed as if they were possessions or objects: 'such rooms, so many servants and so splendid a dinner' (p. 133) whereas at Pemberley the housekeeper plays a small but important role praising Mr Darcy. She says, 'There is not one of his tenants or servants but what will give him a good name' (Vol. 3, Ch. 1, p. 204).

VOLUME 2, CHAPTERS 8–10: GENTLEMEN VISITORS

SUMMARY

- Elizabeth enjoys a lively, intelligent conversation with Colonel Fitzwilliam which attracts attention from Mr Darcy and Lady Catherine.

- Mr Darcy moves away from Lady Catherine to listen to Elizabeth's piano playing.

- Darcy and Elizabeth tease one another as they talk with Colonel Fitzwilliam.

- Mr Darcy visits the Parsonage when Elizabeth is alone. He is awkward and silent.

- Colonel Fitzwilliam takes care to warn Elizabeth that he needs to marry someone wealthy. He also tells her that Darcy recently saved his friend Bingley from a 'most imprudent marriage' (p. 153).

WHY ARE THESE CHAPTERS IMPORTANT?

A Seeing how easily Elizabeth talks to Colonel Fitzwilliam evidently gives Darcy confidence in his romance. He sees that Elizabeth is well able to cope in **upper-class society**: 'You cannot have been always at Longbourn,' Darcy says (p. 149). At this moment in the novel she does not understand what a serious obstacle her **family** is.

B The **theme** of **marriage as an economic arrangement** is mentioned by Colonel Fitzwilliam, who is aware he has come close to flirting with Elizabeth. She is privately embarrassed but manages to make a joke of it: 'And pray, what is the usual price of an Earl's younger son?' (p. 152)

C Story **structure**. Colonel Fitzwilliam could not have told Elizabeth about Darcy's interference between Bingley and Jane at a worse moment.

REVISION FOCUS: DARCY AND ELIZABETH

When Charlotte says, 'My dear Eliza he must be in love with you, or he would never have called on us in this familiar way' (p. 149), she is giving the reader a hint. Imagine either that you are in the parlour at Hunsford Parsonage or the drawing room at Rosings and are observing Mr Darcy. What might make you guess he is in love with Elizabeth? Do you have any suspicion that Elizabeth could ever feel the same about him? Jot down your thoughts.

TOP TIP (A01)

When writing about the marriage theme, don't forget Colonel Fitzwilliam. It is surprising to discover that he too will be marrying for money. His obvious admiration for Elizabeth may help convince the reader as well as Darcy how genuinely attractive and charming she is.

VOLUME 2, CHAPTER 11: DARCY PROPOSES

SUMMARY

- Elizabeth is too upset by Colonel Fitzwilliam's revelation to go to Rosings. She stays alone at the Parsonage re-reading Jane's letters and noticing her sister's depression.
- Darcy arrives unexpectedly and asks her to marry him.
- This could not have come at a worse moment. She is shocked, flattered, insulted and refuses him.
- When he asks her to explain, she accuses him of ruining Jane's happiness and reducing Wickham to poverty.
- Finally she accuses him of not behaving in a 'gentleman-like manner' (p. 160).

WHY IS THIS CHAPTER IMPORTANT?

A Powerful expression of Darcy's **passion, pride** and **awkwardness**.

B An opportunity for Elizabeth to express all the **resentment, false impressions** and **unacknowledged emotion** that she has been suppressing.

C This chapter is a crucial development in the **romance** and is also central to the **themes** of **marriage, pride, manners** and **class**.

KEY CHARACTER: DARCY (A01)

Austen has been working towards this moment ever since Darcy began to notice Elizabeth's 'fine eyes' (Vol. 1, Ch. 6, p. 21). She has frequently presented him as unnaturally silent (for example on several of his visits to the Parsonage) and has expressed his inner conflict through his movements. Here he sits down, stands up, walks round the room, stays silent, then obviously makes up his mind. 'He came towards her in an agitated manner, and thus began, "In vain I have struggled. It will not do. My feelings will not be repressed. You must allow me to tell you how ardently I admire and love you"' (p. 156). If you compare this to Mr Collins claiming to be 'run away with his feelings' (Vol. 1, Ch. 19, p. 88) you will see how effectively Austen has established Darcy as a genuinely passionate man. 'Ardently' is a word that has connotations of fire and burning. It contrasts with Elizabeth's 'cold' civility at this point (p. 156). Unfortunately he also speaks with 'warmth' (p. 157) about his contempt for her family. Throughout *Pride and Prejudice* Darcy develops more than any other **character** and this is the halfway stage in his journey.

TOP TIP (A02)

If you compare this proposal with Mr Collins's or with other examples of Darcy and Elizabeth's dialogue you will see that the hero and heroine are adept at using the same language: for example here they both accuse each other of incivility (p. 156). This reveals the essential understanding and shared values which, in the end will make them a good couple. Darcy listens to Elizabeth as Mr Collins never did.

KEY THEME: MANNERS

Although Darcy's pride is his downfall here, the real problem is the amount of time he spends talking about Elizabeth's background. He is proud of being 'honest' (p. 159) but Elizabeth is quick to point out that he has simply been rude. He has focused on explaining his own feelings and has failed to notice that he is hurting hers. This lack of sensitivity is bad manners. However, she too chooses to disregard normal politeness ('the established mode') when she tells him that she is not grateful for his proposal (p. 157). He accuses *her* of rudeness 'so little *endeavour* at civility' and she replies that he was rude first (p. 158). She says that his lack of politeness about her family has spared her 'the concern which I might have felt in refusing you, had you behaved in a more gentleman-like manner' (p. 160). We later discover that this is the phrase that really hurts Darcy and makes him change. It is important to notice, however, that his rudeness is in *expressing* his feelings about her family, not in *thinking* them. In fact Elizabeth will soon discover that she agrees with him.

TOP TIP

Notice the unusually high number of negative compound words in this scene of misunderstanding and rejection. Find some of the words beginning with the prefix 'un-' and consider what effect they have (pp. 156–60).

EXAM FOCUS: MAKING LINKS

It is important to be able to make links across the novel. Read this example by a student which links Darcy's proposal scene with the previous chapter:

> Jane Austen uses free indirect speech to allow the reader into Elizabeth's mind so that we share her thoughts and feelings about Darcy's proposal. In the previous chapter we saw how alive she was to the idea of marriage when Colonel Fitzwilliam explained why he couldn't propose to someone with no fortune and Elizabeth understood what he was telling her: 'Is this,' thought Elizabeth, 'meant for me?'

Link reveals key plot development

Now you try it:

Conclude this paragraph by analysing Elizabeth's shock at Darcy's proposal, including 'the tumult of her mind' at the end of the chapter.

VOLUME 2, CHAPTERS 12–13: A TURNING POINT FOR ELIZABETH

SUMMARY

- Darcy is waiting for Elizabeth on her morning walk in the park. He hands her a letter and leaves.
- This letter explains his actions concerning Bingley and Wickham. He admits that he thought Jane was indifferent to Bingley.
- He criticises members of Elizabeth's family for their 'want of propriety' (p. 164) and then explains Wickham's true nature and his attempt to elope with Darcy's sister, Georgiana, when she was fifteen years old. Georgiana's fortune is thirty thousand pounds.
- Elizabeth reads, re-reads and begins to rethink.

WHY ARE THESE CHAPTERS IMPORTANT?

A The letter is as important to **Elizabeth's development** as a character as her refusal of his proposal was to Darcy. She becomes **ashamed** of her overhasty judgments and her **prejudices**.

B Wickham's true nature is revealed and the themes of **marriage** and **money** emphasised yet again.

C The importance of correct **social behaviour** is mentioned and the question of how far an individual should be judged by the actions of their **family**.

> **TOP TIP** (A02)
>
> Highlight some of the words Austen uses to describe Elizabeth's 'perturbed state of mind' at the beginning of Chapter 13 (p. 169). This will help you to focus on the language Austen uses to convey characters' emotions.

KEY THEME: PREJUDICE (A02)

Elizabeth begins to read 'With a strong prejudice against every thing he might say' (p. 169) but Darcy has appealed to her 'justice' instead of her 'feelings' (p. 162). Her first reading of the letter is emotional but crucially she takes it out and reads it again more carefully and rationally. She 'commanded herself so far as to examine the meaning of every sentence' (p. 170 – a good tip!). This time she is not judging on first impressions. She realises how prejudiced she has been.

KEY LANGUAGE: USE OF NEGATIVES (A02)

At first Elizabeth tells herself that Darcy's and Wickham's conflicting stories are both 'only assertion' (p. 170) but then realises how little she knows of Wickham's background. She was convinced by his charm, good looks and local popularity. Now she realises how wrong it was of him to tell her such a story on first meeting and how wrong she had been to listen. Austen uses a string of negative words to express both the wrongness of Elizabeth's behaviour and, more important (for the later development of the story), the falseness and untrustworthiness of Wickham: 'impropriety', 'indelicacy', 'inconsistency', 'no fear', 'no reserves', 'no scruples' (p. 171).

KEY QUOTATION: ELIZABETH'S MOMENT OF TRUTH (A01)

'She grew absolutely ashamed of herself. – Of neither Darcy nor Wickham could she think, without realising that she had been blind, partial, prejudiced, absurd' (p. 172). This is Elizabeth's moment of truth and she makes no excuses for herself. She is 'absolutely ashamed'. Her capacity for honesty and her ability to change is what entitles her to be the heroine of this novel.

AIMING HIGH: AUSTEN'S SOCIAL WORLD ⭐

Check back over the moments when a new character is introduced. There is often a surprisingly large amount of information concerning their money or their relatives. This reflects the smaller social world of Jane Austen's times. Strangers were less common than they are today and proper introductions were important. Somehow Wickham has slipped through this protective net. It is not only Elizabeth who has been fooled by him – so has the 'neighbourhood' (p. 171). And the neighbourhood judged Darcy wrongly too, when he first appeared at the Meryton Assembly. Austen supports social conventions (such as correct introductions) but often satirises the changing nature and mistakes of public opinion.

TOP TIP (A02)

Analyse Elizabeth's speech beginning 'How despicably have I acted!' and ending 'Till this moment I never knew myself' (pp. 172–3). Underline the key words that show her change of heart. Notice the extraordinary string of exclamations. This is quite unlike her usual sentence style.

VOLUME 2, CHAPTERS 14–17: HOME TO LONGBOURN

SUMMARY

- Darcy and Fitzwilliam leave and Elizabeth prepares to return home – ignoring Lady Catherine's interference.
- She re-reads Darcy's letter whenever she is alone and thinks about her own behaviour and the faults of her family.
- Mr Collins tells her how happy he is with Charlotte. Elizabeth can see that Charlotte is still glad to have a home of her own.
- Elizabeth and Maria Lucas travel to the Gardiners' house in London. They collect Jane and set out for Hertfordshire.
- On the journey, they stop at a coaching inn where they meet Kitty and Lydia. Lydia tells them that the Militia are moving to Brighton. She is determined to go too.
- At Longbourn, Mr Bennet is relieved to see Elizabeth and at last she has a chance for a private talk with Jane.
- Jane is shocked by all she hears and they agree to keep their knowledge about Wickham's true character a secret.

WHY ARE THESE CHAPTERS IMPORTANT?

A The **change in Elizabeth's attitudes and feelings** is revealed in more detail.

B Charlotte's **marriage choice** is looked at again.

C There are clues about the **future development** of the **plot**.

KEY CHARACTERS : THE BENNET FAMILY

Elizabeth has been away from her family and forced to look at them in a different light. She even blames her father for failing to control her younger sisters. The narrator, however, allows us to glimpse Mr Bennet's relief that Elizabeth is home again. There is much more focus on Lydia in this section – her noisiness, public bad behaviour, selfishness and insensitivity.

TOP TIP: WRITING ABOUT APPEARANCE AND REALITY

'How much I shall have to tell!' says Maria as they leave Hunsford. Elizabeth privately adds, 'And how much I shall have to conceal' (p. 180). The difference between appearance and reality is a major theme of fiction and there are many ways to consider it in this novel. For example, it is a feature of style, with irony often the gap between what is said and what is meant. Austen suggests that secrecy is a way of surviving social life – behaving politely and keeping your thoughts to yourself, as Elizabeth does with Lady Catherine.

KEY CONTEXT A03

Lady Catherine says, 'Why at that rate you will only have been here six weeks. I expected you to stay two months' (p. 175). In Austen's time long visits to other people's houses were quite usual – partly because travel was so difficult.

A01

A01

VOLUME 2, CHAPTERS 18–19: LYDIA'S TRIUMPH

SUMMARY

- Lydia is invited to accompany Colonel Forster and his wife to Brighton.
- Elizabeth attempts to persuade her father not to allow Lydia to go.
- Elizabeth meets Wickham and hints at what she has learned of his past.
- Lydia departs and Elizabeth thinks about her parents' marriage.
- The Gardiners cannot take Elizabeth to the Lake District as planned. Instead they set off for Derbyshire and decide to look at Pemberley.

WHY ARE THESE CHAPTERS IMPORTANT?

A Elizabeth's new understanding of the collective importance of **family** encourages her to try to persuade her father to keep Lydia at home. Mr Bennet shows his laziness as a **parent** – as well as his personal love and respect for Elizabeth.

B There is a focus on Lydia's **character**.

C Mr and Mrs Gardiner are included as positive representations of **marriage** and **family**.

KEY THEMES: MARRIAGE AND FAMILY (A02)

The narrator describes the incompatible marriage of Mr and Mrs Bennet, based on physical attraction alone. Elizabeth is shown to be aware of her father's deficiencies as a parent. Previously his love for her and her respect for his intelligence has persuaded her not to mind too much. However recent events have convinced her that his failure to take responsibility affects all of them. By contrast, the Gardiners are an example of a good marriage.

AIMING HIGH: SETTING AND STRUCTURE

Chapters 18–19 focus on some of the worst aspects of life at home with the Bennet family. These chapters, between Elizabeth's encounters with Darcy in Kent and Derbyshire, serve as a domestic interlude. The fact that the most emotionally significant events take place away from Longbourn emphasises the independence of her inner life. Her eventual move to become mistress of Pemberley reflects how she has outgrown the confines of Longbourn.

TOP TIP (A01)

Austen presents two different sides to Lydia in Chapter 18 – a fun-loving teenager 'tenderly flirting with at least six officers at once' (p. 192) and a danger to the family: 'the very great disadvantage to us all, which must arise from the public notice of Lydia's unguarded and imprudent manner' (pp. 190–1). How do you view Lydia at this stage in the novel?

CHECKPOINT 11 (A01)

Why was it a mistake for Elizabeth and Jane to conceal the truth about Wickham?

VOLUME 3, CHAPTER 1: PEMBERLEY AT LAST

SUMMARY

- At Pemberley the Gardiners and Elizabeth are filled with admiration at its combination of natural beauty and good taste.
- They meet the housekeeper, Mrs Reynolds, who has known Darcy since childhood and praises his fine qualities.
- Darcy appears. Both he and Elizabeth struggle to overcome their embarrassment.
- He meets them again, deliberately. Elizabeth introduces him to her aunt and uncle. He invites Mr Gardiner fishing then asks Elizabeth if he can introduce her to his sister.
- Elizabeth is confused and amazed.

WHY IS THIS CHAPTER IMPORTANT?

A The housekeeper's testimony sheds new light on Darcy's character. His behaviour to Elizabeth and members of her family immediately suggests how much he has changed since their last encounter.

B Pemberley is presented as an ideal setting.

KEY CONTEXT (A03)

When this novel was written, taste was changing from formal gardens and landscape to complete wildness. In literature this was expressed by the Romantic movement (e.g. by the poet William Wordsworth) as a desire to be emotionally moved by natural beauty. Elizabeth and the Gardiners clearly share this but also admire the earlier, eighteenth-century fashion for landscaping – shaping nature into man-made parks and views.

TOP TIP: WRITING ABOUT DARCY (A01)

The almost complete absence of characters from different social classes in *Pride and Prejudice* makes Austen's decision to use the housekeeper significant. 'I have never had a cross word from him in my life, and I've known him since he was four years old,' she says (p. 203). Her list of Darcy's good qualities includes his devotion to his sister, generosity to the poor and excellence as a master and landlord.

KEY SETTING: PEMBERLEY (A02)

Austen rarely uses much space describing locations for their own sake. The descriptions of Rosings, for example, are memorable mainly for the comic effect of Elizabeth listening to Mr Collins numbering the fields and trees in each direction – 'every view was pointed out with a minuteness that left beauty entirely behind' (Vol. 2, Ch, 5, p. 130) – and give an impression of materialism. In contrast, the approach to Pemberley is seen through Elizabeth's eyes and her responses are interwoven with each new sight. The journey takes her from the woods, into the park then reveals an eye-catching view of the house: 'Elizabeth ... had never seen a place for which nature had done more, or where natural beauty had been so little counteracted by an awkward taste ... at that moment she felt, that to be mistress of Pemberley might be something!' (p. 200)

EXAM FOCUS: ANALYSING BODY LANGUAGE (A02)

When you are analysing the way Austen communicates physical emotion you need to consider the part played by body language. Read this example by a student:

> The reader may have guessed that Elizabeth and Darcy will meet while she is at Pemberley but Austen manages the encounter apparently casually, placing it in the middle of a paragraph where Mr Gardiner is trying to estimate the date of the building. This is contrasted with the heightened emotion shown in Elizabeth and Darcy's blushes and how Darcy – 'absolutely started' and then stands completely still for a moment. However self-control is one of Darcy's key qualities and Austen shows that he is much better able to control himself that he was in Hunsford Parsonage. He manages 'perfect civility' if not 'perfect composure'. The balance of language reflects his success in keeping calm.

Good observation of author's use of structure

Shows overall understanding of Darcy's character

Effective use of verbal detail and its effect

Now you try it:

Write a further paragraph analysing Elizabeth's body language. Begin: *Elizabeth is not so successful....*

VOLUME 3, CHAPTER 2: ELIZABETH'S HOPES RISE

SUMMARY

- Darcy, his sister (Georgiana) and Bingley arrive much sooner than expected. Everyone does their best to be friendly.
- Elizabeth and the Gardiners are invited to dine at Pemberley.
- When alone, Elizabeth is overcome with gratitude towards Darcy for loving her well enough to forgive her previous rejection and unjust accusations.

TOP TIP

Notice that Elizabeth has learned to be much more careful when forming first impressions. She has been told that Georgiana Darcy is 'exceedingly proud' but she doesn't rush to judge her. She looks more carefully and discovers that she is 'only exceedingly shy' (p. 213).

WHY IS THIS CHAPTER IMPORTANT?

A There is a sense that events are taking a **turn for the better**.

B Elizabeth's **outlook** becomes more **positive**.

KEY CONTEXT: MANNERS AND SOCIAL CONVENTIONS

The **conventions** of Austen's time enabled relationships to progress at a careful pace. Understanding of the conventions was shared between members of a social class. For instance, the Gardiners are quick to notice that the Darcys have called sooner than normal. Being invited to dine at Pemberley is a significant step forward in friendship so Mrs Gardiner is anxious to know whether Elizabeth is comfortable with this. Good manners include being careful not to intrude into other people's private feelings. The Gardiners are a good example of this sensitivity (unlike Lady Catherine or Mrs Bennet): 'They saw much to interest, but nothing to justify enquiry' (p. 216).

TOP TIP

You can make your own writing more effective by varying the types and lengths of sentences.

KEY LANGUAGE: SENTENCE STRUCTURES

Austen's longer sentences are clearly organised by use of subclauses and/or rhetorical balance: for example 'and more than commonly anxious to please, she [Elizabeth] naturally suspected that every power of pleasing would fail her' (p. 213). Thus far Elizabeth has seemed able to behave very easily and naturally as well as politely, so this complex sentence expresses her new self-consciousness. The three-part sentence 'Bingley was ready, Georgiana was eager, and Darcy determined to be pleased.' (p. 214) is held together by pattern and rhythm as the three visitors are held together by their wish to be friends. Use of long sentences means that any very simple sentence stands out, for example: 'It was gratitude' (p. 217).

VOLUME 3, CHAPTER 3: POOR MISS BINGLEY

SUMMARY

- Elizabeth and Mrs Gardiner pay an awkward visit to Pemberley.
- Caroline Bingley shows her jealousy and criticises Elizabeth as soon as she has left. Darcy snaps and praises Elizabeth.

WHY IS THIS CHAPTER IMPORTANT?

A Themes of **manners**, true **politeness** and **sensitivity** are explored.

B Caroline Bingley's **jealousy** makes Darcy say what he really thinks.

TOP TIP: WRITING ABOUT ABOUT MANNERS **A02**

Here contrasting characters reveal themselves by their good manners or otherwise. A strained atmosphere is eased only by the polite conversation of Mrs Gardiner and Miss Darcy's paid companion, Mrs Annesley. Caroline Bingley cannot resist making a thinly disguised reference to Wickham which mainly hurts Georgiana. Later Caroline criticises Elizabeth's appearance in specific detail: 'She is grown so brown and coarse!' (p. 222) Notice her list of Elizabeth's bad qualities (face, complexion, features, nose, teeth, etc.). Despite her social status and good education, Caroline is not a truly refined person. In contrast, Darcy can 'contain himself no longer' and states how much he admires Elizabeth in respectful terms: 'it is many months since I have considered her as one of the handsomest women of my acquaintance.'

KEY LANGUAGE: THE NARRATOR'S VOICE **A02**

The narrator often explains people's behaviour: for example, Georgiana's shyness could make people assume she was proud, especially if they 'felt themselves inferior' (p. 219). The narrator also comments on people's behaviour, pointing out that Caroline has only succeeded in making Darcy say 'what gave no one any pain but herself' (p. 223). Jane Austen's ironic tone can invite us to smile at characters' behaviour in an affectionate way as well as a satirical or judgemental way. Her description of Mrs Gardiner and Elizabeth presents them as slightly comic but is not unkind: 'Mrs Gardiner and Elizabeth talked of all that had occurred, during their visit, [...] except what had particularly interested them both' (p. 223).

CHECKPOINT 12 **A01**

Study what Miss Bingley says about Elizabeth in Volume 3, Chapter 3. Where else in the novel does she show her dislike by commenting on her appearance?

VOLUME 3, CHAPTERS 4–6: BAD NEWS

SUMMARY

- Elizabeth receives letters from Jane saying that Lydia has eloped.
- Darcy arrives as she is reading them, is obviously upset but says very little except to express his concern and promise secrecy.
- Elizabeth is certain that this family disgrace will finally end her relationship with Darcy. She realises how much she 'could have loved him' (p. 228). Now all she wants is to get home to help Jane.
- The Gardiners find it hard to believe that Lydia and Wickham will not marry but Elizabeth has no confidence in Lydia and knows what Wickham is really like.
- Mr Bennet has gone to London and Mrs Bennet is hysterical.
- Lydia's letter to Mrs Forster presents her elopement as a huge joke.
- Mr Gardiner goes to London. Mr Collins sends a letter. Mr Bennet returns home.

WHY ARE THESE CHAPTERS IMPORTANT?

A A new, dramatic twist to the **plot** – events begin to justify Elizabeth's worries about Lydia. This is Austen's neat way of bringing together themes of **love and marriage** and **families and behaviour**.

B Elizabeth and Darcy's **romance** was going too smoothly. Now there is **tension** as Darcy is keeping his feelings to himself and events are happening off stage, which Elizabeth doesn't know about (and neither do we).

C The weakness of the Longbourn **family** is highlighted.

TOP TIP (A02)

Note Austen's description of body language is not only connected with physical attraction. Here Elizabeth's feelings make it impossible for her to speak but her pale colour and her 'impetuous manner' help Darcy to see that there is something badly wrong. Follow Austen's description of Elizabeth's movements on p. 226.

CHECKPOINT 13 (A01)

What makes the family begin to worry that Wickham does not plan to marry Lydia?

KEY STRUCTURE: THE IMPORTANCE OF LETTERS (A02)

Many of the letters in this novel are mentioned but not included – such as the letters from Mr Gardiner, who thoughtfully keeps his wife up to date with events, unlike Mr Bennet. However, there are also key letters that move the story on: for example the letters from Jane with the shocking news. There are also letters which further reveal characters, such as the letter from Lydia exclaiming, 'What a good joke it will be!' (p. 239). Mr Collins's letter underlines the seriousness of the situation for the other sisters: 'For who, as Lady Catherine herself condescendingly says, will connect themselves with such a family' (p. 244). Fortunately there is narrative irony in this, as the answer to Lady Catherine's question is ... her own nephew!

KEY CONTEXT (A03)

Pride and Prejudice contains a very large number of letters. This is not surprising since letters were an essential means of communication at that time. Also Austen had enjoyed reading 'epistolary novels' which consisted of letters only.

EXAM FOCUS: MRS BENNET AS CARICATURE (A01)

Austen presents Mrs Bennet as a caricature incapable of thinking about anyone except in relation to herself. Read this example by a student exploring this aspect of Mrs Bennet and her effect on others:

> Jane Bennet is the kindest and most unselfish person in the novel and therefore suffers the most from her mother's behaviour. From the beginning of the story we have been told that Mrs Bennet feels unwell when anything upsets her so it is no surprise when Jane tells Elizabeth, 'My poor mother is really ill and keeps to her room.' Elizabeth understands at once that this means Jane has had to manage everything as their sisters are almost equally selfish. We learn that 'Mary studies so much, that her hours of repose should not be broken in on'.
>
> Even when Mrs Bennet imagines her husband being killed in a duel she is only worried about herself and being turned out of Longbourn. This is a reasonable fear but within a few sentences she is equally anxious about Lydia's clothes. We can infer that she has no moral standards or sense of proportion.

Good link back to the start of the novel

Useful quotation because it tells the reader as much about Jane's generous nature as about Mary's studiousness

Shows personal interpretation

Now you try it:

Write another paragraph looking at Mr Bennet's reaction. Begin: *Mr Bennet's reaction to the crisis is predictably different ....*

VOLUME 3, CHAPTERS 7–8: THE COST OF A WEDDING

SUMMARY

- Mr Gardiner writes, saying that Lydia and Wickham have been found and proposing a monetary settlement to guarantee their marriage.
- Mrs Bennet is overjoyed and begins to make extravagant plans for Lydia.
- Mr Bennet realises that someone must have secretly paid Wickham a very much larger sum. He assumes this is Mr Gardiner.
- Wickham will join a new regiment and he and Lydia will make a fresh start in the North of England. Mr Bennet is finally persuaded to allow them to visit Longbourn on their journey.

WHY ARE THESE CHAPTERS IMPORTANT?

A This is the most explicit statement of the link between **marriage** and **money**.

B We see how **vulnerable** Lydia's **position** is.

KEY QUOTATION: 'TEN THOUSAND POUNDS!' (A02)

Mr Bennet knows more of the world than Jane and Elizabeth and realises immediately that Mr Gardiner is not telling him the full details of the settlement: 'Wickham's a fool, if he takes her with a farthing less then ten thousand pounds' (p. 250). Jane and Elizabeth are shocked: 'Ten thousand pounds! [...] How is half such a sum to be repaid?' (p. 250) It is obvious from Mr Bennet's attitude that he knows he will never be able to repay this amount. None of them guess the truth. They are also shocked that this huge sum of money has had to be spent in order for Lydia to marry 'one of the most worthless young men in Great Britain' (p. 253). Mrs Bennet's response is predictably shallow: now that her daughter has been saved from disgrace she makes plans to go out visiting her neighbours again and spend more money on clothes and a large house for the newly weds.

KEY CONTEXT: THE PRESSURE TO MARRY (A03)

The story of Lydia and Wickham's elopement challenges our modern understanding. Given that Lydia has reached today's age of consent (sixteen) it may not seem so shocking that a teenage girl might have sex outside marriage, and so the idea of bribing her partner to marry her seems surprising. However, Lydia has no means of stopping herself getting pregnant and if Wickham were to leave her there would be no guaranteed financial help for her. Even without a child, once she has lost her virginity and her good name, prostitution would be almost the only way in which she could support herself. That is what is meant by 'come upon the town' (p. 254).

VOLUME 3, CHAPTERS 9–10: AN UNEXPECTED GUEST

SUMMARY

- Lydia and Wickham arrive cheerfully at Longbourn.
- Lydia reveals that Darcy was at the wedding. Jane is too polite to ask more as this should have been a secret. Elizabeth decides to write to Mrs Gardiner.
- Mrs Gardiner's reply tells Elizabeth that it was Darcy who settled Wickham's debts and therefore bribed him to marry Lydia.
- Darcy claims that this was because he should have revealed Wickham's true character but Mrs Gardiner hints that love for Elizabeth was his real motive.
- Elizabeth ensures Wickham will not spread any more false stories about Darcy. She makes clear that she knows the truth of his actions.

WHY ARE THESE CHAPTERS IMPORTANT?

A We learn more about Lydia's **character** and **behaviour**.

B Darcy's **involvement** prepares us for **new developments**.

KEY CHARACTER: LYDIA BENNET **A01**

Austen emphasises the unsatisfactory nature of Lydia's wedding and arrival at Longbourn by considering it from Jane or Elizabeth's point of view: 'Jane more especially, who gave Lydia the feelings that should have attended herself had *she* been the culprit, was wretched in the thought of what her sister must endure' (p. 259). This emphasises the comic surprise of Lydia's arrival: 'Lydia was Lydia still; untamed, unabashed, wild, noisy and fearless' (p. 259). She, like Mrs Bennet, is a character who is incapable of development. Others, even her sister Kitty, have the capability to learn and to change. Lydia boasts of her married state, declaring that she now takes precedence over Jane at the table and offering to 'get husbands' for her sisters. '"I thank you for my share of the favour," said Elizabeth; "but I do not particularly like your way of getting husbands"' (p. 261).

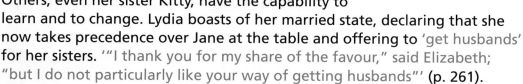

KEY QUOTATION: FAMILY TIES **A02**

Elizabeth could make trouble for Wickham but he is now part of her family: 'Come, Mr Wickham, we are brother and sister, you know. Do not let us quarrel about the past' (p. 271). This shows family as a strong concept and the idea of reconciliation prepares us for the happy ending of the novel too.

TOP TIP **A01**

Go through the novel and find all the scenes involving Lydia. Make notes on how she resembles her mother.

VOLUME 3, CHAPTERS 11–13: BINGLEY RETURNS TO NETHERFIELD

SUMMARY

- Wickham and Lydia leave for Newcastle and Bingley is rumoured to be returning to Netherfield. Mr Bennet says he will not visit.
- Bingley visits the Bennets accompanied by Darcy.
- Elizabeth is nervous of facing Darcy but pleased that Bingley is attentive to Jane.
- On their next visit Bingley shows increasing affection towards Jane but Darcy is distant and soon departs for London.
- Bingley proposes to Jane; she accepts and Mr Bennet gives his permission.

WHY ARE THESE CHAPTERS IMPORTANT?

A There is **tension** and **suspense**, despite events suggesting a **good outcome**.

B The **plotline** of Bingley and Jane's relationship is **resolved**.

C Darcy and Elizabeth's story seems to take a **new twist**.

KEY CHARACTER: MR WICKHAM (A02)

This is the last time that Wickham will appear directly. He says goodbye to the Bennets with great charm: 'He smiled, looked handsome, and said many pretty things' (p. 272). Mr Bennet re-interprets this as 'smirks' and 'simpers'. He then explicitly compares Mr Wickham to Mr Collins. Both men were introduced at the same point in the story but while Mr Collins was understood to be stupid and conceited even before he arrived, Wickham appeared charming and likeable at first. Elizabeth and the reader have learned that they were wrong to judge him by his attractive appearance. Underneath he is completely false – more so than Mr Collins.

AIMING HIGH: MAKING COMPARISONS

As the novel reaches its conclusion, it is worthwhile looking back at the opening chapters. In some ways, this episode is a repeat. Elizabeth and Darcy meet face to face but this time there are no witty remarks. The proud Mr Darcy, who has been attracted to Elizabeth from the outset, is overcome with shyness, while the previously self-confident Elizabeth can feel only doubt and despair. Comparing the two situations with suitable quotations or supporting detail is known as cross-referencing and may gain you extra marks.

VOLUME 3, CHAPTERS 14–15: LADY CATHERINE IS 'MOST SERIOUSLY DISPLEASED'

SUMMARY

- Lady Catherine arrives at Longbourn. She demands that Elizabeth denies that she is engaged to Darcy and promises never to enter such an engagement.
- Elizabeth refuses.
- Mr Collins writes to Mr Bennet advising him that Lady Catherine will never give her consent to 'so disgraceful a match' (p. 300).
- Mr Bennet thinks this is 'delightfully absurd' (p. 301) and can't understand why Elizabeth is not amused.

WHY ARE THESE CHAPTERS IMPORTANT?

A The scene with Lady Catherine is **dramatic** and makes an important contribution to the **theme** of **manners**, **social class** and **true equality**. 'He is a gentleman; I am a gentleman's daughter' (p. 295), Elizabeth tells her.

B Elizabeth and her father have always been united by their sense of **humour**. He has not noticed how she has changed: 'Never had his wit been directed in a manner so little agreeable to her' (p. 300). She is suffering as Jane suffered from their mother's tactless comments about Bingley.

CHECKPOINT 14 (A01)

What has triggered Lady Catherine's unexpected visit?

KEY LANGUAGE: DIALOGUE (A02)

The confrontation between Lady Catherine and Elizabeth is one of the most strongly written passages of **dialogue** in the novel. Lady Catherine, who prides herself on her 'sincerity and frankness' (p. 292) shows herself to be arrogant and insulting. Elizabeth defends herself by listening carefully to whatever Lady Catherine says and turning it back on her. For example when Lady Catherine asks whether Darcy has made Elizabeth an offer of marriage, Elizabeth is able to avoid giving a direct answer: 'Your ladyship has declared it to be impossible' (p. 293). However, when Lady Catherine says that Elizabeth will pollute 'the shades of Pemberley' Elizabeth has had enough: 'You have insulted me, in every possible method' (p. 296). Lady Catherine is so angry that she refuses to say goodbye: 'I take no leave of you, Miss Bennet. I send no compliments to your mother. You deserve no such attention' (p. 297). The rhythmical repetition of 'no ... no ... no' is intended to emphasise her anger but only reveals her lack of real power.

It is well worth looking at the strong sentence rhythms in this chapter as well as examples of other literary devices such as **alliteration**, when Lady Catherine accuses Elizabeth of using her 'arts and allurements' (p. 293) to draw Darcy in. Though this is obviously rude, it is little different from the way Charlotte suggested earlier that Jane ought to behave to succeed in 'fixing' or to 'secure' Bingley (Vol. 1, Ch. 11, p. 16).

TOP TIP (A01)

References to a particular scene may serve more than one purpose. For example, if you are writing about Mr Collins you might want to refer to the section where he proposes to Elizabeth. But this scene can also tell you a lot about Elizabeth's character.

AIMING HIGH: LINKING WORDS

There is a revealing moment when Mr Bennet says, 'For what do we live but to make sport for our neighbours, and laugh at them in our turn?' (p. 301) This may remind you of the moment when Elizabeth tells Darcy how much she enjoys a joke: 'Follies and nonsense, whims and inconsistencies *do* divert me, I own, and I laugh at them whenever I can' (Vol. 1, Ch. 11, p. 46). The linking word is 'divert'. Now, in this awkward conversation, Mr Bennet asks Elizabeth whether she is amused by Mr Collins's suggestion that Mr Darcy might be attracted to her. She claims she is 'excessively diverted' (p. 301) but it is not true. She has discovered that there are more serious reasons for existence than laughing at other people, even Mr Collins.

VOLUME 3, CHAPTERS 16–17: 'THAT DISAGREEABLE MR DARCY'

SUMMARY

- Bingley brings Darcy to Longbourn and the young people go for a walk.
- Elizabeth thanks Darcy for helping Lydia. He confesses he did it for her.
- He asks if her feelings remain the same as at Rosings. She admits they have completely changed. He proposes and is accepted.
- They discuss their turbulent relationship and how they came to realise they loved each other.
- The Bennets are amazed at Elizabeth's news – each in their own way.

WHY ARE THESE CHAPTERS IMPORTANT?

A   The final affirmation of **romance**. Elizabeth, the heroine, has won love, **marriage** and **money** by her intelligence, honesty – and attractiveness. Her willingness to admit her mistakes and change has been her most outstanding quality.

B   Darcy, the hero, has also admitted his mistakes and changed. The **themes** of **manners**, good **class** and proper **pride** (not snobbery) reach a conclusion here.

C   **Family** issues remain. Jane and Mrs Bennet react in characteristic ways – Mr Bennet goes further. He truly loves Elizabeth and for once takes her happiness seriously: 'My child, let me not have the grief of seeing *you* unable to respect your partner in life' (p. 312).

KEY THEME: PRIDE AND PREJUDICE (A02)

This theme reappears as Elizabeth and Darcy confess their mistakes. Darcy admits being deeply hurt by her justified accusation that he had not behaved in a 'gentleman-like' manner (p. 304). He explains how his upbringing had made him proud and selfish even though his parents were good people. He is truly grateful to her for forcing him to change: 'You taught me a lesson, hard indeed at first, but most advantageous. By you, I was properly humbled' (p. 306). In return she tells him how important his letter was in forcing her to think again and gradually removing 'all her former prejudices' (p. 305).

TOP TIP: WRITING ABOUT THE ENDING (A01)

Focus on how the events are not only romantic but comic. Fear and hope transform clear-headed Elizabeth into a blushing young woman, while Darcy becomes a tongue-tied suitor. Mrs Bennet's disgust evaporates at the prospect of Darcy's large income. Mr Bennet is suddenly serious while Elizabeth teases Jane about loving Darcy for 'his beautiful grounds at Pemberley' (p. 309). The connection of marriage and money, initially threatening, has almost become a joke.

TOP TIP (A02)

Elizabeth knows her mother will be either violently set against the match or violently delighted. Notice how Austen springs a small surprise: Mrs Bennet is silent. After that her speech is even more fragmented than usual, full of incomplete sentences and exclamation marks.

VOLUME 3, CHAPTERS 18–19: A HAPPY ENDING

SUMMARY

- Elizabeth learns that Darcy admires her lively mind and that his reticence on recent visits to Longbourn was due to embarrassment. She admits to the same sensation and they rejoice in recalling how the ice was finally broken.

- Replies are sent to Mr Collins's, Lady Catherine's and Mrs Gardiner's letters.

- The Collinses arrive at Lucas Lodge to escape Lady Catherine's ill temper. So Darcy has to endure Mr Collins as well as Mrs Philips and Mrs Bennet. Elizabeth longs for the 'comfort and elegance' (p. 318) of Pemberley.

- Jane and Elizabeth are married on the same day. The narrator tells us what happens to everyone else.

WHY ARE THESE CHAPTERS IMPORTANT?

A They provide a **review** and **commentary** on the novel's characters and events.

B Austen briefly maps out the characters' **futures**.

REVISION FOCUS: LOOSE ENDS

Austen gives a summary of the characters and their future situations. Mrs Bennet, despite having her wildest dreams fulfilled, remains as silly as ever, but the lives of all members of the families are altered in some way by the marriages. Make a table with three columns listing whose lives and characters improve, whose become more difficult and who remains unchanged by events.

TOP TIP: WRITING ABOUT THE CONCLUSION (A01)

CHECKPOINT 15 (A01)

What makes the ending happy for Mary Bennet?

This romantic novel may seem to have a simple 'happy ever after' ending but you should relate this to its wider themes. The final chapter mirrors a society which has achieved a state of relative peace and stability. After misunderstanding and turmoil, old prejudices have been banished by the formation of new alliances. Some things cannot be improved. Neither Mrs Bennet nor Lady Catherine will achieve true gentility and the Wickhams will continue to pursue their flimsy dreams, but Pemberley appears to offer a glimpse of an ideal world. You may feel that Austen's decision to end with the focus on the Gardiners is an effective way of linking the themes of a good marriage, responsible family members and true gentility.

PROGRESS AND REVISION CHECK

SECTION ONE: CHECK YOUR KNOWLEDGE

Answer these quick questions to test your basic knowledge of the novel, its characters and events:

1. Who is desperate to marry off her daughters at the start of the novel?

2. Who is described as 'so odd a mixture of quick parts, sarcastic humour, reserve, and caprice' (Vol. 1, Ch. 1)?

3. At the first ball, how many times does Bingley dance with Jane?

4. Who shows her jealousy of Elizabeth as Mr Darcy tries to write a letter?

5. Who prefers playing backgammon to reading on his visit to Longbourn (Vol. 1, Ch. 13–14)?

6. Who charms Elizabeth on his first appearance (Vol. 1, Ch. 15–17)?

7. The Bennets are the last to leave Netherfield on the night of the ball. What does Lydia do?

8. Who cannot believe Elizabeth when she refuses his offer of marriage?

9. What might Elizabeth's reaction to her first sight of Miss de Bourgh tell us about her feelings towards Darcy?

10. What is suggested by Mr Darcy and Colonel Fitzwilliam's visit to Hunsford Parsonage so soon after their arrival at Rosings?

11. Who moves closer when Elizabeth is playing the piano in Volume 2, Chapter 8?

12. Who uses a letter to explain his actions concerning Bingley and Wickham?

13. How much money did Wickham take from Darcy when he decided he did not want to become a clergyman?

14. Who treats Jane and Elizabeth to lunch but tells them they will have to lend the money as 'we have just spent ours at the shop out there' (Vol. 2, Ch. 16, p. 181)?

15. Where is Lydia invited to go by Colonel and Mrs Forster?

16. Who tells Elizabeth that Mr Darcy 'was always the sweetest-tempered, most generous-hearted, boy in the world' (Vol. 3, Ch. 1, p. 203)?

17. Who criticises Elizabeth's appearance for a second time in the novel?

18. How does Elizabeth hear about Lydia and Wickham's elopement?

19. Who arrives at Longbourn in a chaise and four and demands to speak to Elizabeth?

20. Who marry on the same day?

PROGRESS AND REVISION CHECK

SECTION TWO: CHECK YOUR UNDERSTANDING

Here are two tasks on the significance of particular moments in the novel. These require more thought and slightly longer responses. In each case, try to write at least three to four paragraphs.

Task 1: In Volume 2, Chapter 8, in what ways is the section in which Elizabeth plays the piano significant? Think about:

- How it reveals the prejudice of Lady Catherine
- The changing relationship of Mr Darcy and Elizabeth

Task 2: In Volume 2, Chapters 18–19, why is the section in which Elizabeth tries to persuade her father not to let Lydia go to Brighton important? Think about:

- What we learn about Elizabeth's changing attitude to her father
- What we learn about her family in general

PROGRESS CHECK

GOOD PROGRESS

I can:

- Understand how Austen has sequenced and revealed events. ☐
- Refer to the importance of key events in the novel. ☐
- Select well-chosen evidence, including key quotations, to support my ideas. ☐

EXCELLENT PROGRESS

I can:

- Refer in depth to main and minor events and how they contribute to the development of the plot. ☐
- Understand how Austen has carefully ordered or revealed events for particular effects. ☐
- Draw on a range of carefully selected key evidence, including quotations, to support my ideas. ☐

WHO'S WHO?

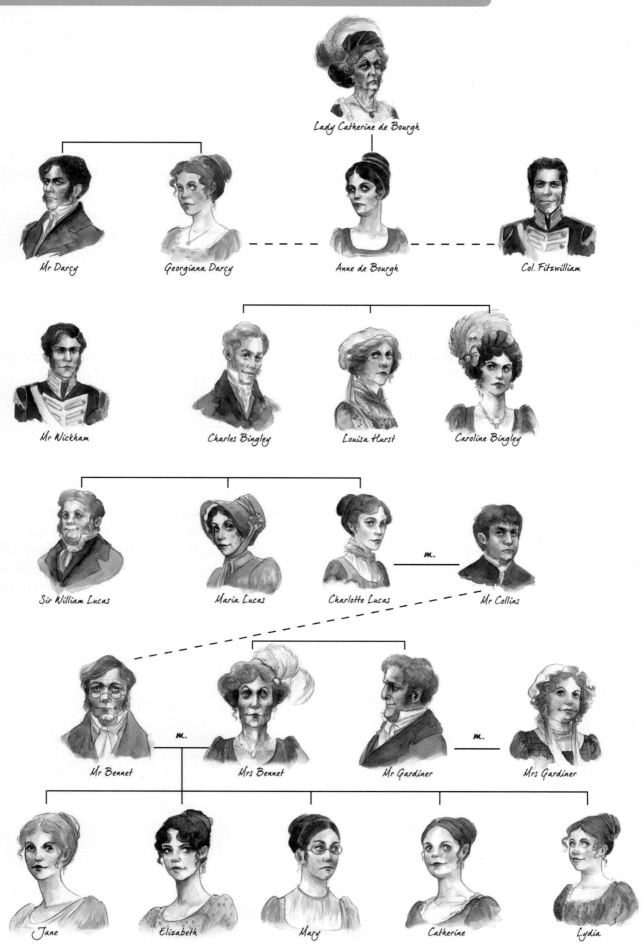

Lady Catherine de Bourgh

Mr Darcy

Georgiana Darcy

Anne de Bourgh

Col. Fitzwilliam

Mr Wickham

Charles Bingley

Louisa Hurst

Caroline Bingley

Sir William Lucas

Maria Lucas

Charlotte Lucas

m.

Mr Collins

Mr Bennet

m.

Mrs Bennet

Mr Gardiner

m.

Mrs Gardiner

Jane

Elizabeth

Mary

Catherine

Lydia

ELIZABETH BENNET

ELIZABETH'S ROLE IN THE NOVEL

Elizabeth Bennet is the second eldest of the five Bennet sisters, who at the beginning of the novel are all unmarried. She is the heroine and events are frequently viewed from her perspective. In the novel, she:

- meets Darcy at a local ball and immediately takes a dislike to him
- rejects Mr Collins's proposal of marriage, even though acceptance would guarantee financial security for herself and a future home for others in her family
- is immediately charmed by the handsome Wickham and believes his account of ill treatment by Darcy
- refuses Darcy's first offer of marriage and accuses him of not being 'gentleman-like' (Vol. 2, Ch. 12, p. 160)
- begins to revise her opinions on reading Darcy's letter of explanation; later visits Pemberley, Darcy's estate, and finds she has been completely mistaken about him
- resists Lady Catherine's attempts to bully her and marries Darcy on the same day as her sister Jane marries Darcy's friend Bingley.

TOP TIP (A01)

It is often revealing to see a character from another character's point of view. Elizabeth is the first of the Bennet sisters named in the novel. Her father offers to 'throw in a good word' for her (Vol. 1, Ch. 1, p. 2). Her mother is offended and describes her in negative terms – 'not half so handsome as Jane, nor half so good-humoured as Lydia.' Her father mentions her quality of 'quickness'. Here we learn what different qualities the Bennet parents value as well as getting to know the novel's heroine.

ELIZABETH'S IMPORTANCE TO THE NOVEL AS A WHOLE

As the central character of the novel it is through Elizabeth's eyes that we see the vast majority of events. She is capable of making mistakes and wrong judgements but is intelligent, self-critical and capable of development. She is lively and observant as well as sensitive but restricted by her family and her neighbourhood and by the absence of opportunities for a young lady of her class. You may enjoy Elizabeth's dialogue and admire her for being quick enough to defend herself while (usually) remaining polite. Elizabeth and the narrator often seem very close in their attitudes and Austen presents her sympathetically even when she is wrong. However strong Charlotte Lucas's sensible arguments on marriage, it is Elizabeth's romance that dominates the story.

EXAM FOCUS: WRITING ABOUT ELIZABETH

Key point	Evidence
● Elizabeth is less immediately attractive or less fun loving than some of her sisters, though she has a strong sense of humour.	● 'she is not half so handsome as Jane, nor half so good humoured as Lydia' (Vol. 1, Ch. 1, p. 2). ● 'I dearly love a laugh' (Vol. 1, Ch. 11, p. 46).
● When necessary, she is prepared to be unladylike and unconventional.	● 'Elizabeth continued her walk alone, crossing field after field at a quick pace, jumping over stiles' (Vol. 1, Ch. 7, p. 26).
● Darcy recognises that her expressive face reveals a lively mind.	● Her face 'was rendered uncommonly intelligent by the beautiful expression of her dark eyes' (Vol. 1, Ch. 6, p. 17).
● She has the intelligence and wisdom to gain Darcy's respect.	● 'You taught me a lesson [...] By you I was properly humbled' (Vol. 3, Ch. 16, p. 306).
● Elizabeth is observant. The reader often watches her watching others and shares her feelings.	● At the Netherfield ball 'had her family made an agreement to expose themselves as much as they could [...] it would have been impossible for them to play their parts with [...] finer success' (Vol. 3, Ch 18, p. 85).

TOP TIP: WRITING ABOUT ELIZABETH AS HEROINE (A01)

Make sure you explain how Austen places Elizabeth at the centre of the novel. Focus on key aspects of her character and where they are most clearly illustrated: her lively intelligence (Vol. 1, Ch. 11–12); her strong-mindedness (Vol. 1, Ch. 19; Vol. 2, Ch. 11; Vol. 3, Ch. 14); her readiness to acknowledge her misjudgements (Vol. 2, Ch. 13; Vol. 3, Ch. 1–2); her embarrassment about her family (Vol. 1, Ch. 18; Vol. 3, Ch. 4–6). Also make clear how often other characters and events are seen from Elizabeth's point of view – which is often very close to the narrator's (Vol. 1, Ch. 10; Vol. 2, Ch. 5).

REVISION FOCUS: ELIZABETH'S CHANGE OF HEART

To help you track the way Austen develops Elizabeth's character ask yourself these questions:

● Why does she take against Darcy so quickly? Why is she so ready to believe Wickham? Why does she reject Darcy's first proposal? (How often has she felt shame for her family before Darcy gives his point of view?)

MR FITZWILLIAM DARCY

MR DARCY'S ROLE IN THE NOVEL

Mr Darcy is a rich landowner who has a higher social status than any other character in the novel. He is the nephew of Lady Catherine de Bourgh and is the novel's hero. In the novel, he:

- first appears with his friend Bingley at a public ball in Meryton
- becomes attracted to Elizabeth while she is visiting Jane at Netherfield
- reappears when Elizabeth is visiting her friend Charlotte in Kent; asks Elizabeth to marry him but she rejects him
- welcomes Elizabeth and the Gardiners at his country estate, Pemberley
- rescues Lydia from disgrace by arranging a regimental post for Wickham and paying his debts
- eventually returns to Longbourn, proposes once again and is accepted.

EXAM FOCUS: WRITING ABOUT MR DARCY

Key point	Evidence
● Darcy commands attention with his good looks, distinguished manner and wealth.	● He 'drew the attention of the room by his fine, tall person, handsome features, noble mien; and the report [...] of his having ten thousand a year' (Vol. 1, Ch. 3, p. 7).
● His silence and superior manner can give offence.	● 'the proudest, most disagreeable man in the world' (Vol. 1, Ch. 3, p. 7).
● He is strongly attracted to Elizabeth but aware of the difference in their social status.	● Elizabeth 'attracted him more than he liked' (Vol. 1, Ch. 12, p. 48).
● His housekeeper, Mrs Reynolds, gives a different perspective on her employer.	● 'He is the best landlord, and the best master [...] that ever lived [...] Some people call him proud; but I am sure I never saw any thing of it' (Vol. 3, Ch. 1, p. 204).
● Darcy is self-controlled and often silent. Austen frequently uses description of body language to suggest his hidden feelings.	● 'His complexion became pale with anger, and the disturbance of his mind was visible in every feature' (Vol. 2, Ch. 11, p. 158).

TOP TIP: WRITING ABOUT DARCY AS HERO (A02)

Think about Darcy as a romantic hero (if you know *Jane Eyre* by Charlotte Brontë you could compare him to Mr Rochester). He is a man of the world and seemingly unobtainable for a small-town girl – 'To be mistress of Pemberley might be something!' (Vol. 3, Ch. 1, p. 200) Darcy is conscious of his social standing and appears self-assured, which can be interpreted as arrogant and unfriendly (Vol. 2, Ch. 8, pp. 145–6). He is quick witted enough to put down those who should know better – though he is usually self-controlled unless pushed too far (e.g. by Miss Bingley, Vol. 3, Ch. 3, p. 222).

There is a hidden side to Darcy, revealed when Elizabeth visits Pemberley (Vol. 3, Ch. 1–3) and when he is confident enough to reveal his true feelings (Vol. 3, Ch. 16). He possesses a strong sense of duty, as shown in his protective care of his sister, his good management of his estate (Vol. 3, Ch. 1) and in his steps to rescue the situation of Lydia and Wickham (Mrs Gardiner's letter, Vol. 3, Ch. 10, pp. 264–8).

KEY QUOTATION: DARCY'S FIRST PROPOSAL (A02)

Darcy's first, unsuccessful proposal is anything but cool: 'My feelings will not be repressed. You must allow me to tell you how ardently I admire and love you' (Vol. 2, Ch. 11, p. 156). Austen successfully presents Darcy as a man of strong feelings (ardent) who can usually keep his passion in check (repressed). It makes a clever contrast with 'the fire and independence' of Mr Collins's character – which is an example of the **narrator** using **sarcasm** (Vol. 1, Ch. 22, p. 101).

KEY QUOTATION (A02)

Ensure you understand how marriage is inextricably linked to money. This is made clear from the novel's opening sentence onwards: 'It is a truth universally acknowledged, that a single man in possession of a good fortune, must be in want of a wife' (Vol. 1, Ch. 1, p. 1).

JANE BENNET

JANE BENNET'S ROLE IN THE NOVEL

Jane (Miss Bennet) is the eldest and most beautiful of the five sisters. She and Elizabeth are particularly close and are always able to speak honestly to each other though their characters are contrasted. In the novel, Jane:

- dances with Bingley at the first ball and they are immediately attracted
- is invited by Bingley's sisters to Netherfield, where she falls ill and is visited by Elizabeth
- is invited to London by the Gardiners and hopes to meet Bingley again, but is hurt and disappointed when she receives only a single visit from Miss Bingley
- accepts Bingley's offer of marriage when he eventually returns to Netherfield.

TOP TIP: WRITING ABOUT JANE (A01)

Contrast Jane with Elizabeth and also with Charlotte Lucas when writing about the theme of marriage. It would be impossible for Jane ever to scheme to catch a husband. Her misplaced trust in Caroline Bingley leaves her unsuspecting of the true reasons for Bingley's absence (Vol. 1, Ch. 21).

EXAM FOCUS: WRITING ABOUT JANE (A01)

Key point	Evidence
• Jane is gentle and credits people with good reasons for their actions.	• 'her mild and steady candour always pleaded for allowances' (Vol. 2, Ch. 1, p. 115).
• She takes an optimistic view of the human race.	• 'poor Jane! who would willingly have gone through the world without believing that so much wickedness existed in the whole race of mankind' (Vol. 2, Ch. 17, p. 185).
• She protects herself so effectively that most people do not notice what she is feeling.	• 'My mother means well; but she does not know, no one can know how much I suffer from what she says' (Vol. 3, Ch. 11, p. 274–5).

MR CHARLES BINGLEY

MR BINGLEY'S ROLE IN THE NOVEL

Mr Bingley is a rich young man whose money has been made in trade. This means he does not have the land, responsibilities or social standing of his friend Mr Darcy. He has two sisters: one (Louisa) is married, the other (Caroline) is single. In the novel, he:

- rents Netherfield Park and brings his sisters and friend to stay with him there
- is attracted to Jane Bennet as soon as they first dance together
- has little self-esteem (the good side of pride) so it is easy for Darcy to persuade him that Jane does not care for him; he rushes away from Netherfield as unexpectedly as he has arrived
- is not fickle, although he is hasty; he continues to love Jane and wastes no time in proposing to her as soon as he knows she has loved him all along.

EXAM FOCUS: WRITING ABOUT BINGLEY (A01)

Key point	Evidence
He is friendly, approachable, kindly and well mannered.	'He is just what a young man ought to be,' says Jane Bennet (Vol. 1, Ch. 4, p.10).
His attraction to Jane is immediate and lasting.	'he could not imagine an angel more beautiful' (Vol. 1, Ch. 4, p. 12).
He is more likely to turn to Darcy than to trust himself. This is the other side of his modesty and easy-going nature.	'Upon my word I cannot exactly explain the matter, Darcy must speak for himself.' (Vol. 1, Ch. 10, p. 40).

TOP TIP: WRITING ABOUT BINGLEY (A01)

Bingley's arrival at Netherfield sets the whole story in motion and is the occasion for the famous opening sentence about eligible bachelors. When thinking about the predatory approach to marriage Austen implies – Mrs Bennet's behaviour is a prime example of this – we might feel some sympathy for Mr Bingley. Darcy has a protective attitude to his friend, as explained by Colonel Fitzwilliam (Vol. 2, Ch. 10); but we also know how much pain Jane suffers because of Darcy's interference. Notice how Bingley and Darcy are compared and contrasted from their first appearance (Vol. 1, Ch. 3, p. 7) and also when Elizabeth is staying at Netherfield (Vol. 1, Ch. 8–11). Bingley is always easier to like but Elizabeth is right to think his easiness may make him weak (Vol. 3, Ch. 16, p. 308) – he is easily persuaded and influenced by his friend.

TOP TIP (A01)

Compare Bingley's friendship with and respect for Darcy with Wickham's attitude. Wickham has no real friends or background and is isolated in the novel as a result.

MR AND MRS BENNET

THE ROLE OF MR AND MRS BENNET IN THE NOVEL

Mr Bennet is a gentleman farmer whose estate provides an income of two thousand pounds per year but which will go to his cousin when he dies. **Mrs Bennet** is a tradesman's daughter with little money of her own. They live at Longbourn and have five daughters.

In the novel **Mr Bennet**:

- is clever and amusing but not easy to live with. In the first chapter he pretends that he won't visit Mr Bingley but does. He is always ready to mock or tease his wife in front of his daughters and later humiliates his daughter Mary in public.
- allows Mr Collins to visit the house partly so that he can laugh at him
- generally plays a role in the novel defined by what he does not do. He criticises his younger daughters for running after officers but does nothing to stop them. He loves Elizabeth but does not listen to her nor understand or comfort Jane in her distress. He has never saved money so cannot help Lydia.

In the novel **Mrs Bennet**:

- is excited by the news that Mr Bingley is coming to Netherfield as she is desperate to find husbands for her daughters
- is quite undiscriminating so is equally glad to welcome Mr Collins (once she has got over her prejudice)
- sees nothing wrong with Mr Wickham's character once he and Lydia are actually married.
- is very shallow and changeable – note her treatment of her friend Lady Lucas for instance
- is usually seen from the point of view of Jane or Elizabeth, who find her behaviour embarrassing in public and insensitive in private.

TOP TIP: WRITING ABOUT MR AND MRS BENNET (A01)

Mr and Mrs Bennet are incompatible. She doesn't understand him: he understands and despises her. Later we are told that they married as a result of a physical attraction which did not last. Can we infer that Lydia and Wickham's marriage will go the same way?

TOP TIP (A01)

The final scene between Elizabeth and her father (Vol. 3, Ch. 17, pp. 311–12) is essential to understanding his character and is crucially relevant to the theme of marriage.

MR WILLIAM COLLINS

MR COLLINS'S ROLE IN THE NOVEL

Mr Collins is a Church of England rector who will inherit Mr Bennet's estate. His patron is Lady Catherine de Bourgh, Darcy's aunt. He arrives in the story at almost the same moment as Mr Wickham. In the novel, he:

- invites himself to Longbourn as prospective inheritor of Mr Bennet's estate. He is ready to marry and plans to make an offer to one of the girls – if they are as attractive as he has heard.
- proposes to Elizabeth (as Jane is not available) and, when rejected, proposes to her friend Charlotte Lucas a few days later
- talks all the time about his patroness Lady Catherine de Bourgh and sees it as his job to flatter her.
- is delighted to announce that they are all invited to dine with Lady Catherine when Elizabeth and the Lucases visit Charlotte in her new home
- writes to Mr Bennet condemning Lydia's behaviour and expressing relief that he didn't marry Jane or Elizabeth so is not part of their disgrace.
- warns against Elizabeth accepting a proposal from Darcy without Lady Catherine's approval. Mr Bennet replies, cynically, 'If I were you I would stand by the nephew. He has more to give' (Vol. 3, Ch. 18, p. 317).

EXAM FOCUS: WRITING ABOUT MR COLLINS (A01) ✏

Key fact	Evidence
● He is pompous, self-important, hypocritical and rather stupid. He grovels to Lady Catherine.	● 'He was a tall, heavy looking young man of five and twenty. His air was grave and stately' (Vol. 1, Ch. 13, p. 53).
● Elizabeth and her father see through him immediately.	● '"Can he be a sensible man, sir?" "No, my dear; I think not [...] There is a mix of servility and self-importance in his letter which promises well"' (Vol. 1, Ch. 13, p. 52).

KEY QUOTATION: MARRIAGE AND MR COLLINS (A02)

Mr Collins finds it hard to believe that Elizabeth has rejected him: 'and you should take it into farther consideration that in spite of your manifold attractions, it is by no means certain that another offer of marriage may ever be made to you' (Vol. 1, Ch. 19, p. 91). His tone is almost threatening and forces us to understand the risk Elizabeth is taking by saying no, even to such an unattractive and ridiculous character.

MR GEORGE WICKHAM

MR WICKHAM'S ROLE IN THE NOVEL

Mr Wickham is an outwardly charming young man whose father served Darcy's father on the Pemberley estate. If this novel has a human villain, it is Wickham. In the novel, he:

- meets the Bennet sisters when they have walked to Meryton with Mr Collins
- is immediately attractive
- uses his charm to fool Elizabeth into believing he was wronged by Darcy, who later explains that Wickham had tried to run away with his fifteen-year-old sister for the sake of her fortune
- develops a relationship with Elizabeth but when a Miss King inherits a large sum of money switches his attention to her
- elopes with Lydia. He does not intend to marry her but is persuaded to do so by Darcy, who pays his debts and buys him a commission in a new regiment.

TOP TIP: WRITING ABOUT MR WICKHAM   **A01**

Wickham could be seen as a version of the romantic hero, the handsome stranger who enters the plot to sweep the heroine off her feet. In fact he is the villain. How might readers guess that they should be on their guard?

EXAM FOCUS: WRITING ABOUT MR WICKHAM   **A01**

Key point	Evidence
● Wickham has the appearance and speech to charm any young woman.	● 'he had all the best part of beauty, a fine countenance, a good figure, and very pleasing address' (Vol. 1, Ch. 15, p. 59).
● Even the clear-sighted Elizabeth is initially won over.	● 'Elizabeth thought with pleasure of dancing a great deal with Mr Wickham' (Vol. 1, Ch. 17, p. 72).
● Jane learns from Bingley that Wickham is not all he seems.	● 'Mr Wickham is by no means a respectable young man' (Vol. 1, Ch. 18, p. 80).
● Wickham's interest in women is purely to do with money.	● 'His attentions to Miss King were now the consequence of views solely and hatefully mercenary' (Vol. 2, Ch. 13, p. 172).
● His lack of feeling and consideration for anyone but himself is confirmed.	● 'Wickham's affection for Lydia, was just what Elizabeth had expected to find it; not equal to Lydia's for him' (Vol. 3, Ch. 9, p. 261).

MINOR CHARACTERS

CHARLOTTE LUCAS

Charlotte is the eldest daughter of Sir William and Lady Lucas, the Bennets' neighbours at Longbourn. She is a plain, sensible woman, 27 years old and not yet married. This worries her brothers, who will have to support her if she remains single, and is also preventing her younger sisters from 'coming out' and having their chance to find a husband. Charlotte is Elizabeth Bennet's particular friend and her role is to present the practical, unromantic view of marriage. She believes 'happiness in marriage is entirely a matter of chance' (Vol. 1, Ch. 6, p. 17) but Elizabeth does not take Charlotte seriously when she advises how Jane should 'secure' Bingley (pp. 16–17). Their friendship is severely tested when Charlotte accepts Mr Collins just a few days after he has been rejected by Elizabeth.

KEY QUOTATION: CHARLOTTE LUCAS (A02)

Charlotte tells Elizabeth, 'I am not romantic you know. I never was. I ask only a comfortable home' (Vol. 1, Ch. 22, p. 105). Elizabeth's long visit to Hunsford Parsonage (Vol. 2, Ch. 5–15) enables her and the reader to notice some of the strategies by which Charlotte makes her home comfortable – such as persuading her husband to take up gardening. Charlotte and Elizabeth's friendship is repaired but it will never be the same and Elizabeth feels ever closer to her refined and sensitive sister Jane. Although we can infer that Charlotte has made the best choice she can, Elizabeth and Jane will make marriages that offer romance as well as a 'comfortable home'.

LYDIA BENNET

Lydia is the youngest of the five Bennet sisters – fifteen years old at the start of the novel. Her main importance is to the **theme** of marriage, which she appears to take extremely lightly, ignoring Wickham's financial position – the polar opposite of Charlotte Lucas. Clearly she is physically attracted to him but could have been equally attracted to any officer in the regiment. A trip to Brighton 'comprised every possibility of earthly happiness [...] she saw herself seated beneath a tent, tenderly flirting with at least six officers at once' (Vol. 2, Ch. 18, p. 192). Lydia is presented as loud, assertive and impolite. She harasses Bingley for a ball (Vol. 1, Ch. 9, p. 36), yawns in public (Vol. 1, Ch. 8, p. 86) and spends the money for her sisters' meal on a bonnet that she does not even like (Vol. 2, Ch. 16, p. 181).

She is important to the theme of family too since her bad behaviour damages the reputation of Jane and Elizabeth. When she finally elopes with Wickham she may have ruined her sisters' chances of marriage 'for who, as Lady Catherine condescendingly says, will connect themselves with such a family' (Vol. 3, Ch. 6, p. 244). Lydia's letter describing her marriage as 'a good joke'

TOP TIP (A01)

Never overlook Jane Austen's minor characters. Charlotte's father, Sir William Lucas, is a kindly but comic character. He has been knighted for his services as Mayor of Meryton and his life has changed from that day. He tries to behave as a gracious courtier but is completely overawed by wealth and power when he meets Lady Catherine de Bourgh.

(Vol. 3, Ch. 5, p. 239) reveals her lack of seriousness, but also that she did expect to marry Wickham – whereas he had no intention of marrying her. Lydia behaves with particular insensitivity towards Jane (Vol. 3, Ch. 9, p. 260) and is not a character who has the capacity to learn or change: 'Lydia was Lydia still; untamed, unabashed, wild, noisy, and fearless' (p. 259). It is not surprising that she is her mother's favourite child as they are very much alike.

CAROLINE BINGLEY

Caroline demonstrates that money, education, fine clothes and accomplishments do not necessarily make someone refined or sensitive. She and her sister Louisa 'could describe an entertainment with accuracy, relate an anecdote with humour, and laugh at their acquaintance with spirit' (Vol. 1, Ch. 11, p. 43). This is a typical example of Austen's **style** where a pattern of three phrases is used to lure the reader towards a moral judgement – notice how Caroline often begins talking about someone as soon as they have left the room and has just been heard making unkind fun of the Bennets to Mr Darcy (p. 42). In contrast, Elizabeth is amused by 'follies and nonsense, whims and inconsistencies' (p. 46) but her laughter is private and not unkind. Caroline becomes a comic figure as she pursues Mr Darcy. Frequently she provokes him into breaking his usual polite silence to reveal his true feelings. When she criticises Elizabeth for being 'brown and coarse' she eventually makes him so angry that he tells her he considers Elizabeth 'one of the handsomest women of my acquaintance' (Vol. 3, Ch. 4, p. 222).

LADY CATHERINE DE BOURGH

Lady Catherine is a key figure in connecting the three volumes. She is first mentioned at Longbourn in Volume 1 by Mr Collins. She has given him his job and he feels it is his duty to repay her in flattery. She is also Mr Darcy's aunt, so when Elizabeth goes to stay with the Collinses in Volume 2 it is perfectly natural for her to meet Mr Darcy there. In Volume 3, Lady Catherine drives from Kent to Hertfordshire to make Elizabeth promise never to become engaged to Mr Darcy. Elizabeth's refusal gives Darcy hope that she may care for him and encourages him to propose again. Elizabeth comments: 'Lady Catherine has been of infinite use, which ought to make her happy, for she loves to be of use.' (Vol. 3, Ch. 18, p. 316) Austen uses many detailed examples to show her interfering in matters that are not her concern, such as Mr Collins's cupboard shelves (Vol. 1, Ch. 14, p. 55), Charlotte's livestock (Vol. 2, Ch. 6, p. 136) and Maria's packing (Vol. 2, Ch. 15, p. 177). Elizabeth can be admired for being 'the first creature who had ever dared to trifle with so much dignified impertinence!' (Vol. 2, Ch. 6, p.138)

TOP TIP (A01)

Don't ignore the other Bennet sisters, Mary and Kitty. The narrator often seems unkind to them, condemning Mary for her efforts to improve herself and Kitty for being weak in following Lydia. Yet it is clear that part of their problem comes from their father's poor parenting skills. Both are given a happy ending and the possibility of change.

TOP TIP: WRITING ABOUT MINOR CHARACTERS (A01)

Notice what minor characters, such as Lady Catherine's daughter Anne and Darcy's sister Georgiana, show about the people who look after them. Anne hardly speaks though her mother and Mr Collins often talk about her, making ridiculous statements about her beauty and potential talent, whereas Elizabeth sees her as 'sickly and cross' (Vol. 2, Ch. 5, p. 132). Georgiana is a more fully developed character. Her brother takes loving care of her though she is too much in awe of him.

PROGRESS AND REVISION CHECK

SECTION ONE: CHECK YOUR KNOWLEDGE

1. Name Mrs Bennet's brother and sister and their spouses (two couples).

2. Who is being described here? 'They were of a respectable family in the north of England' (Vol. 1, Ch. 4, p. 11).

3. Which character links Mr Collins and Mr Darcy?

4. Who is being described here? 'She looks sickly and cross [...] She will make him a very proper wife' (Vol. 2, Ch. 5, p. 132).

5. Mr Wickham tries to elope with two teenage girls. He is unsuccessful with one, successful with the other. Who are they?

6. Was Sir William Lucas born into the upper social classes?

7. Why does Mary Bennet try so hard to be considered accomplished?

8. Who feels it her duty to warn Elizabeth against Wickham?

9. Who says this about Mr Darcy: 'He was always the sweetest-tempered, most generous-hearted, boy in the world' (Vol. 3, Ch. 1, p. 203)?

10. What is Georgiana's most obvious problem, according to Elizabeth?

> **TOP TIP** (A01)
>
> Answer these quick questions to test your basic knowledge of the novel's characters.

SECTION TWO: CHECK YOUR UNDERSTANDING

Task: Discuss Jane Austen's comic presentation of Lydia Bennet. Think about:

- The incident in Meryton when she and Kitty meet Jane and Elizabeth on their return from London
- Her return home as a married woman

> **TOP TIP** (A01)
>
> This task requires more thought and a longer response. Try to write at least three to four paragraphs.

PROGRESS CHECK

GOOD PROGRESS

I can:

- Explain the significance of the main characters in how the action develops. ☐
- Refer to how they are described by Austen and how this affects the way we see them. ☐

EXCELLENT PROGRESS

I can:

- Analyse in detail how Austen has shaped and developed characters over the course of the novel. ☐
- Infer key ideas, themes and issues from the ways characters and relationships are presented by Austen. ☐

THEMES

THEME TRACKER (A01)

Love, marriage and money

- Vol. 1, Ch. 1, p. 1: The marriage–money connection is stated in the first lines of the novel.
- Vol. 1, Ch. 22, p. 105: Charlotte explains her reasons for accepting Mr Collins.
- Vol. 3, Ch. 16, p. 303: Elizabeth and Darcy finally admit their feelings fully.

LOVE, MARRIAGE AND MONEY

Pride and Prejudice can be read as a romantic comedy. Despite the importance of polite behaviour there are many examples of **characters** being influenced by physical attraction.

- Elizabeth dresses 'with more than usual care' and prepares 'in the highest spirits' for an evening dancing with Mr Wickham (Vol. 1, Ch. 18, p. 74) – whom Lydia later describes as 'an angel' (Vol. 3, Ch. 5, p. 239).
- Darcy discovers that his feelings for Elizabeth 'will not be repressed' (Vol. 2, Ch. 11, p. 156).
- Jane feels she is 'the happiest creature in the world' (Vol. 3, Ch. 13, p. 286) when engaged to Bingley, whilst Elizabeth claims she is 'happier even than Jane' (Vol. 3, Ch. 18, p. 317) when she and Darcy have fully acknowledged their feelings for each other.

However, Austen makes it clear that attraction is not enough for a successful marriage:

- Mr Bennet was 'captivated by youth and beauty' but Mrs Bennet's 'weak understanding and illiberal mind' (Vol. 2, Ch. 19, p. 195) soon lost his respect. Mrs Bennet, a tradesman's daughter, has at least captured a gentlemanly husband with a settled income from an estate, but their marriage is not happy.
- Lydia marries with no rational calculation at all. By the end of the novel her and Wickham's relationship is 'unsettled in the extreme' (Vol. 3, Ch. 19, p. 321) and their married life will not be supported by even the financial and social status that her parents enjoy.
- Mrs Gardiner warns Elizabeth against Wickham: 'an affection which the want of fortune would make so very imprudent' (Vol. 2, Ch. 3, p. 120).

Austen presents an unsentimental view of marriage through the character of Charlotte Lucas:

- 'I am not romantic [...] I ask only a comfortable home' (Vol. 1, Ch. 22, p. 105).
- Charlotte asserts that 'happiness in marriage is entirely a matter of chance' (Vol. 1, Ch. 6, p. 17) but at Hunsford Elizabeth notices that she has already adopted various coping strategies such as urging her husband to spend more time in the garden and using a back room to avoid his constant interruptions (Vol. 2, Ch. 7, p. 140).
- Mr Collins's mention of his dear Charlotte's 'situation' (Vol. 3, Ch. 15, p. 301) is a delicate reminder that Charlotte will have had to go to bed with Mr Collins however repulsive she finds him. She is now pregnant.

Securing a happy marriage can be seen as the main objective of the novel, and Austen provides a number of examples:

- Mr and Mrs Gardiner clearly enjoy each other's company (Vol. 2, Ch. 19, p. 198). His 'sensible, gentlemanlike' character is complemented by her 'amiable, intelligent' personality (Vol. 2, Ch. 2, p. 116).

KEY CONTEXT (A03)

Genteel young ladies in Austen's time were expected to be accomplished in music and art. This was partly because they had little to do but was also a way of displaying themselves to potential husbands. Consider how piano playing makes Elizabeth more attractive but Mary less so. Think about other methods of female display – such as when Miss Bingley asks Elizabeth to walk around the room with her to get Darcy to look at them.

- Elizabeth and Mr Bennet approve of Jane and Bingley's marriage because the couple possess a 'general similarity of feeling and taste' (Vol. 3, Ch. 13, p. 287).
- The marriage of Elizabeth and Darcy represents a more complex state of affairs. Their powerful physical attraction has initially included an element of repulsion and they have only achieved mutual understanding and respect through the painful process of deepening self-knowledge and an increase in humility (Vol. 3, Ch. 16).

THE FAMILY AS A SOCIAL UNIT

This theme links to marriage, money, class and pride and gives a useful additional perspective on these central issues.

- Early nineteenth-century society tended to consider the family as a unit. Snobbish Miss Bingley pours scorn on the fact that Jane and Elizabeth's uncle 'lives somewhere near Cheapside' (Vol. 1, Ch. 8, p. 29). This uncle is gentlemanly Mr Gardiner, whom Darcy likes as soon as they are finally introduced (Vol. 3, Ch. 1, p. 209).
- Public bad behaviour by any member of a family can damage the others – as Elizabeth finds at the Netherfield ball (Vol. 1, Ch. 18, p. 85). Although Darcy admits that Jane and Elizabeth are not included in his later criticism, the Bennets' collective 'want of propriety' was one of his strongest reasons for wishing to 'preserve' Bingley from 'a most unhappy connection' (Vol. 2, Ch. 12, p. 164).
- Private bad behaviour – such as Lydia's elopement with Wickham – is even worse. Darcy managed to keep his sister's near-mistake private but Mrs Bennet's uncontrolled hysterics mean that Lydia's story spreads round the neighbourhood in hours. Then 'who, as Lady Catherine herself condescendingly says, will connect themselves with such a family' (Vol. 3, Ch. 6, p. 244). They would pollute 'the shades of Pemberley' (Vol. 3, Ch. 14, p. 296).

AIMING HIGH: WRITING ABOUT FAMILIES IN CONTEXT (A03)

When writing about this theme, you can offer extra insight into what it felt like to live in Jane Austen's time – for example the lack of constant light and heat in every room forced families to spend much more time together, especially in the evenings. Evidence of this can be seen at Longbourn (Vol. 1, Ch. 14), Netherfield (Vol. 1, Ch. 10–11) and Rosings (Vol. 2, Ch. 6 and Ch. 8). Austen suggests that a selfish or insensitive person, like Mrs Bennet, can be a real burden in such constant proximity. Jane suffers most, as Elizabeth points out: 'Your attendance upon her, has been too much for you. You do not look well. Oh! That I had been with you' (Vol. 3, Ch. 5, p. 240).

THEME TRACKER (A01)

The family as a social unit

- Vol. 1, Ch. 18, p. 85: Members of the Bennet family disgrace themselves.
- Vol. 2, Ch. 19, pp. 195–6: Elizabeth pleads with her father.
- Vol. 3, Ch. 1, 8, p. 318: Happily ever after – 'the comfort and elegance of their family party at Pemberley.'

TOP TIP (A01)

When you are thinking about marriage, family responsibility and the individual, key sections to study are when Elizabeth pleads with her father not to allow Lydia to go to Brighton (Vol. 2, Ch. 18, pp. 190–2) and her thoughts afterwards (Vol. 2, Ch. 19, pp. 195–6).

THEME TRACKER (A01)

Manners and class

- Vol. 1, Ch. 1, p. 2: Visiting Mr Bingley – the importance of correct procedure.
- Vol. 2, Ch. 6, pp. 136–8: Lady Catherine's 'dignified impertinence'.
- Vol. 3, Ch. 14, p. 297: Lady Catherine refuses to send compliments.

MANNERS AND CLASS

The world of *Pride and Prejudice* is a socially narrow world.

- Focus is on a few leisured families whose interaction with each other is regulated by conventions such as the need for a correct introduction (Vol. 1, Ch. 1, p. 2). It's necessary to understand these **conventions** in order to assess the significance of characters' actions. For example Miss Bingley's false friendship is made clear by her slowness in replying to Jane's letter (Vol. 2, Ch. 3, p. 123).
- Characters are graded by the amount of money they possess and whether this comes from land (Mr Darcy, Mr Bennet) or trade (the Bingleys, Lucases, Philipses, Gardiners).
- True gentility is demonstrated by behaviour. In a revealing scene, Elizabeth and her aunt visit Georgiana Darcy, who is too shy to speak. The wealthy Mrs Hurst and Miss Bingley do nothing. Only the paid companion helps. The narrator comments that her 'endeavour to introduce some kind of discourse, proved her to be more truly well bred than either of the others' (Vol. 3, Ch. 3, p. 219).

AIMING HIGH: EXPLORING MANNERS AND CLASS

In the example above, Austen speaks through the **narrator** to make her point directly. Generally she allows her characters to reveal themselves. Bad manners are conceit, selfishness, insensitivity and are as apparent in the socially superior Lady Catherine as in Mrs Bennet and Lydia. When Lady Catherine claims that Elizabeth is unsuitable to marry Darcy on the grounds of class, Elizabeth finally speaks out – 'He is a gentleman; I am a gentleman's daughter' (Vol. 3, Ch. 14, p. 295) – and makes her resentment clear: 'You have insulted me, in every possible method' (p. 296).

THEME TRACKER (A01)

Pride and prejudice

- Vol. 1, Ch. 3: Darcy and Elizabeth's first meeting.
- Vol. 1, Ch. 5: The Bennets and Lucases discuss different aspects of pride.
- Vol. 2, Ch. 13: Elizabeth is ashamed of herself.
- Vol. 3, Ch. 16, p. 306: Darcy admits he has been 'properly humbled'.

PRIDE AND PREJUDICE

To trace the significance of the two terms in the title, start at the Meryton Assembly and the conversations afterwards between Bennets and Lucases (Vol. 1, Ch. 3–5).

- Darcy's silence prejudices the neighbourhood against him. He offends Elizabeth's pride by describing her as 'tolerable' (p. 8).
- Charlotte Lucas suggests that Darcy 'has a *right* to be proud' (p. 14). She is referring to a sense of self-esteem and self-confidence, which are good qualities in moderation.
- Snobbery (Lady Catherine), 'superciliousness' (Miss Bingley, Vol. 1, Ch. 6, p. 15) and 'self-importance' (Mr Collins, Vol. 1, Ch. 13, p. 52) are aspects of pride which Austen **satirises** without mercy.

The original title of *Pride and Prejudice* was *First Impressions* and the story shows how hasty judgement leads to prejudice.

● Prejudice may be due to judging by appearance as Elizabeth does when she first meets Wickham (Vol. 1, Ch. 15, p. 59).

● Jane is sensitive and careful whereas Elizabeth is over-confident: '"One does not know what to think." "I beg your pardon; – one knows exactly what to think"' (Vol. 1, Ch. 17, p. 71).

● Darcy's growing attraction forces him to revise his opinion: 'No sooner had he made it clear [...] that she had hardly a good feature in her face, than he began to find that it was rendered uncommonly intelligent by the beautiful expression of her dark eyes' (Vol. 1, Ch. 6, p. 17).

● Elizabeth is much slower and her realisation is painful: 'She grew absolutely ashamed of herself' (Vol. 2, Ch. 13, p. 172).

● Darcy has to learn to know himself better: 'I was given good principles, but left to follow them in pride and conceit' (Vol. 3, Ch. 16, p. 305).

EXAM FOCUS: WRITING ABOUT THEMES A01

Austen's main themes, such as pride and prejudice, are often apparent in quite minor scenes as well as the more obvious set pieces. Read this analysis by a student of Mrs Bennet's visit to Netherfield:

> **[Clear and succinct opening point]** Mrs Bennet has been prejudiced against Darcy ever since he failed to dance with Elizabeth at the Meryton Assembly. She is also comically proud of her locality – there is no evidence that she has ever lived anywhere else. Therefore when Darcy makes a comment about the relative lack of 'intricate characters' in a country neighbourhood Mrs Bennet takes offence. "'Yes indeed" [she cried] "I can assure you that there is quite as much of *that* going on in the country as in the town.'" She probably isn't quite clear what 'intricate' means; Mrs Bennet's conversation is usually confined to domestic details, local gossip and herself. **[Comments on how characters are differentiated by their use of language]** Austen uses silence effectively as she shows Darcy looking at Mrs Bennet for a moment, then turning away. **[Good interpretation]** His movement reveals his contempt but Mrs Bennet assumes she has won a 'victory'. Her aggressive attitude towards such an eligible man as Darcy, is surprising as well as rude and shows the extent of her prejudice and also her wounded pride. **[Picks up on key theme]**

Now you try it:

Write a further paragraph on how other characters respond. Begin: *The reaction of the other characters... .*

CONTEXTS

JANE AUSTEN'S LIFE AND FAMILY

Jane Austen was born in 1775 in Steventon, Hampshire, where her father, George, was rector. Her eldest brother followed their father into the Church. Two of her other brothers, Francis and Charles, were in the Navy and her brother Henry was in the Militia. The deepest bond in her life was with her slightly older sister Cassandra and, as with Jane and Elizabeth in *Pride and Prejudice*, her sister was her closest friend. Neither of them married. They were not financially secure and they and their mother depended on their brothers for support after their father died. Jane Austen's own position was therefore not unlike that facing the Bennet women if none of the girls gained financial support by marriage before their father died. Austen herself could have chosen to marry for security, like Charlotte Lucas, but she did not.

Austen began writing in her teens. One of her first novels was *Lady Susan*, probably written when she was eighteen or nineteen. *First Impressions* was written in 1796, rejected by a publisher in 1797, later rewritten as *Pride and Prejudice* and finally published in 1813. Austen wrote five other major novels, *Sense and Sensibility*, *Northanger Abbey*, *Mansfield Park*, *Emma* and *Persuasion*. In her late thirties, for the first time in her life she was earning money that was her own. She died in 1817.

GENDER AND SOCIAL CLASS

The different roles and opportunities available to men and women were an issue for Austen in her own life. In the novel Elizabeth is exceptional in her capacity for independent thought and action, though she remains a dutiful daughter. Austen knew a wider range of women and a wider social world than is reflected in *Pride and Prejudice* so it is fair to assume that, by insisting on the very limited opportunities available to Elizabeth, she is making a clear artistic point: Elizabeth is exceptional because she is the heroine. The novel's hero Darcy is exceptional too. He is sensitive as well as strong and capable of accepting Elizabeth as his equal, if not superior: 'By you, I was properly humbled [...] You showed me how insufficient were all my pretensions to please a woman worthy of being pleased' (Vol. 3, Ch. 16, p. 306).

CULTURE AND POLITICS

Jane Austen's father had a library of five hundred books and she was encouraged to read widely. She would have used the circulating library as well as reading books in the houses where she lived or visited. Her constant letter writing and sharing other letters written by family and friends kept her much better informed about the wider world than is apparent in *Pride and Prejudice*. She knew about the French Revolution, the war, the slave trade, financial scandals, new plays and books as well as about country poverty, deaths in childbirth, hard domestic drudgery and many other matters that she does not choose to mention. The limitations of the novel are a matter of deliberate choice.

TOP TIP (A02)

Though it was not always easy for Jane Austen to find time and peace in which to write, her close family were supportive and enjoyed listening to her read her work aloud. This is likely to have helped her with the different voices in her dialogue. Reading aloud in your head is a good way to hear her rhythms and understand her sentence structures. To do this, try to 'hear' the words in your head or silently mouth them.

TOP TIP (A01)

One way in which characters are judged is by their attitude to books. Consider this with reference to Mary (Vol. 1, Ch. 2, p. 4), Elizabeth (Vol. 1, Ch. 8, p. 29), Mr Darcy (Vol. 1, Ch. 8, p. 30), Miss Bingley (Vol. 1, Ch. 11, p. 44), Mr Collins and Lydia (Vol. 1, Ch. 14, p. 56).

SETTINGS

Pride and Prejudice is set at the beginning of the nineteenth century, when the Industrial Revolution was in its earliest stages. Most people still lived in small towns or villages. Roads were poor and only the better off were likely to travel for pleasure, as the Gardiners and Elizabeth do in Volume 3.

A change of place in the novel invariably signals a major development in the plot. Settings vary between public (a ball) and domestic (at home). Walks are a useful opportunity to be able to speak more freely.

LONGBOURN AND ITS NEIGHBOURHOOD

The Bennets' home is the centre of the first volume: it is never described from the outside as its appearance would already be familiar to Elizabeth – and her point of view is central to the novel. What is important is the way that Longbourn feels. It is the location for unsatisfactory family life and lacks long-term security. Longbourn is relatively isolated and can be cut off when the weather is bad. Nearby country houses include Netherfield Park and Lucas Lodge; in the small town of Meryton there are some shops, the Assembly Room and Mr and Mrs Philips's home. It is not surprising that the presence of the Militia makes such a difference to Kitty and Lydia.

HUNSFORD PARSONAGE AND ROSINGS PARK

Austen uses much more detail to describe the Collins's and Lady Catherine's homes as her **heroine** (Elizabeth) is seeing them for the first time. Rosings is often described in terms of cost. Generally, however, Austen uses settings to shed light on **characters** and their behaviour. For example when Miss de Bourgh and Mrs Jenkinson stop outside the parsonage, Maria Lucas gets excited, Sir William stands and bows, the Collinses go to the gate and Elizabeth comments that Miss de Bourgh is 'abominably rude to keep Charlotte out of doors in all this wind' (Vol. 2, Ch. 5, p. 132). The secluded walks in Rosings Park offer Elizabeth the chance for a new and relaxed relationship with Colonel Fitzwilliam. Seeing her in a different place helps Darcy to see her in a different light: '*You* cannot have been always at Longbourn' (Vol. 2, Ch. 9, p. 149).

TOP TIP A03

Check the weather in Volume 1. How does it affect the Bennets' daily lives?

PEMBERLEY

Pemberley dominates the third volume although only three chapters take place there. It is presented as ideal in terms of beauty, wealth, taste and social relationships. We have already been prepared by Miss Bingley's scattered comments in Volume 1 but are still able to share Elizabeth's delighted surprise: 'They were all of them warm in their admiration; and at that moment she felt, that to be mistress of Pemberley might be something!' (Vol. 3, Ch. 1, p. 200)

Darcy in his own house seems quite different from Darcy at Netherfield or Rosings. He is quick to introduce Elizabeth to the closest member of his own family, his sister. But Elizabeth can make Pemberley a true family home again (Vol. 3, Ch. 19, p. 321).

Pemberley

Mr Darcy's house

DERBYSHIRE

Rosings

Home of Lady Catherine de Bourgh

Hunsford Parsonage

Mr Collins's house

KENT

Longbourn

The Bennet family's house

HERTFORDSHIRE

Meryton

The nearby village

Netherfield Park

Rented by Mr Bingley

PROGRESS AND REVISION CHECK

SECTION ONE: CHECK YOUR KNOWLEDGE

1. Which two themes are introduced in the first paragraphs?

2. Why is it important that Mr Bennet should call on Mr Bingley?

3. Why are there soldiers in Meryton?

4. What does Mr Collins think is the most beautiful view?

5. Complete this insult and name the speaker: 'Are the shades of _____ to be thus polluted?'

6. Two men in the novel are looking for rich wives. Mr Wickham is one: who is the other?

7. Mr Collins is shocked by the idea of reading a novel to his cousins. What does he choose instead?

8. What does Sir William Lucas describe as 'a charming amusement for young people' (Vol. 1, Ch. 6, p. 19)?

9. Why will Mr Bennet's cousin, Mr Collins, inherit Longbourn after Mr Bennet's death, rather than Mrs Bennet or the Bennet daughters?

10. Mr Wickham claims that Mr Darcy should have given him 'a most valuable living' (Vol. 1, Ch. 16, p. 65). What is meant by the word 'living' in this context?

TOP TIP (A01)

Answer these quick questions to test your basic knowledge of the themes, contexts and settings of the novel.

SECTION TWO: CHECK YOUR UNDERSTANDING

Task: Examine the theme of class and manners, paying close attention to Caroline Bingley and Louisa Hurst's conversation about Elizabeth in Vol. 1, Ch. 8, pp. 27–8. Think about:

- How Caroline and Louisa behave towards Elizabeth in this extract
- How Austen discusses the theme of class and manners elsewhere in the novel

TOP TIP (A01)

This task requires more thought and a slightly longer response. Try to write at least three to four paragraphs.

PROGRESS CHECK

GOOD PROGRESS

I can:

- Explain the main themes, contexts and settings in the text and how they contribute to the effect on the reader. ☐
- Use a range of appropriate evidence to support any points I make about these elements. ☐

EXCELLENT PROGRESS

I can:

- Analyse in detail the way themes are developed and presented across the novel. ☐
- Refer closely to key aspects of context and setting and the implications they have for the writer's viewpoint, and the interpretation of relationships and ideas. ☐

FORM

NOVEL, PLAY OR ESSAY?

Pride and Prejudice is a novel. Today writing a novel is the most likely choice for an author to make, as the novel has become the dominant literary form, but when Jane Austen was growing up people read essays or even sermons for entertainment. Poetry was also more widely read then than now. (You might like to ask yourself why Jane Austen did not write poetry or sermons.)

- Austen's family were enthusiastic about adapting, producing and acting in plays. The influence of drama can clearly be seen in her skill with dialogue and in her description of characters' movements, which sound almost like stage directions.

- Austen owed part of her literary style to the eighteenth-century tradition of essay writing. Essays were relatively short pieces of prose which might be humorous or didactic (written to teach something) and usually commented on some aspect of behaviour or a social issue. They were primarily read for entertainment and for the pleasure of their clear structure and good style.

- In *Pride and Prejudice* Austen laughs at Mr Collins for reading Fordyce's *Sermons* (a best-selling book of the period).

WHAT TYPE OF NOVEL?

Jane Austen uses elements of several different forms in her novel.

- **The epistolary novel:** This type of novel is written entirely in letters from the characters to one another. Austen is known to have enjoyed the epistolary novels of Samuel Richardson and experimented with this form in her early work. The use of letters in *Pride and Prejudice* may have been influenced by this.

- Richardson's novels could also be described as **novels of sensibility** or sentiment. Another writer Austen admired in this genre was Fanny Burney. Novels of sensibility are often romantic and deal with the triumph of the hero or heroine through their goodness. *Pride and Prejudice* is clearly a development of this type of novel but also moves towards the more realistic novels of the later nineteenth century (by Charlotte Bronte, Charles Dickens).

- **Realism** in novels is the recognition of an actual social situation or problem – such as the limited opportunities, apart from marriage, that were open to young women. There is certainly realism as well as romance in *Pride and Prejudice*.

STRUCTURE

OVERLAPPING PLOTS AND COINCIDENCE

A modern feature of *Pride and Prejudice* is the use of overlapping plots. The main romance runs in parallel with the romance of Bingley and Jane. The marriage of Charlotte and Mr Collins deepens our understanding of the theme of marriage, then Lady Catherine (Rosings, Kent, Vol. 2) provides the vital narrative link between Hertfordshire (Longbourn and Netherfield, Vol. 1) and Derbyshire (Pemberley, Vol. 3).

As one plot line is suspended, another is introduced (typically via a new character such as Wickham or Mr Collins) and we discover the hidden links. Austen uses coincidence – as many novel writers do. It is a neat device to ensure that Mr Bennet's estate is entailed to a pompous clergyman whose living is in the gift of Lady Catherine, who happens to be Darcy's aunt. Also Wickham, the anti-hero who runs away with Elizabeth's sister Lydia, has earlier failed to do the same with Darcy's sister Georgiana. This is yet another coincidence but this is how fictional worlds work: we can see them as an intensification of reality.

LETTERS

The twenty-eight letters in the novel help the story to progress. They tell us about events at which characters were not present; summarise complicated events, such as the search for Wickham and Lydia; and remind us of the influence or role of characters who are not physically present. They also reveal a good deal about character by allowing us to 'hear' different voices, for example Mr Collins or Mr Darcy.

TOP TIP: WRITING ABOUT *PRIDE* AND *PREJUDICE* AS A ROMANTIC NOVEL (A02)

You can look at the structure of *Pride and Prejudice* and identify the now-familiar format of the romantic novel. The heroine, who is lively and attractive but not glamorous, becomes acquainted with the hero, who is, in some way, mysterious or even threatening. She is repulsed but he is captivated. Events and feelings force them apart but we know they are really being drawn together. She is distracted by a false lover, but when his wickedness is exposed her eyes are opened to the hero's virtues. But it all seems too late: there are apparently insuperable obstacles to their being united, until the hero secretly takes decisive action and intervenes.

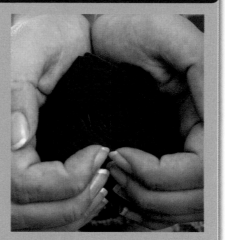

TOP TIP (A02)

Make a list of the novel's key episodes and events and link them to the locations where they happen.

LANGUAGE

OVERVIEW

Jane Austen's narrative style has sometimes been described as detached. It might also be called polished and precise. When she is writing as the narrator she writes carefully as if she is evaluating her characters, checking the gaps between what they say and what they think, catching the echo of their different voices. Sometimes she is a simple reporter of a character's thoughts and feelings (most often Elizabeth's) but she can also be judgemental, contemptuous, sarcastic or warm and humane, even emotional.

LANGUAGE DEVICE: VOICE

What is voice?	The way a character speaks, or the way in which the narrator speaks to the reader.
Example	Mr Collins's voice portrays his conceit and pomposity. When Mr Bennet sets him talking about Lady Catherine's affability, we continue to hear this tone even though it is being reported indirectly via the narrator: 'And with a most important aspect he protested that he had never in his life witnessed such behaviour in a person of rank – such affability and condescension, as he had himself experienced from Lady Catherine' (Vol. 1, Ch. 14, p. 54).
Effect	It is important to hear the rhythm here – the stress falling on 'important', 'never', 'life', 'rank', 'himself', etc. Mr Collins's use of many unnecessary words and such a long sentence, simply to say that Lady Catherine has been kind to him, makes the reader begin to doubt both the reality of the kindness and the intelligence of the speaker.

In good dialogue writing you should be able to identify who is speaking from the style of their speech. You will learn to recognise the tone of their voice – as you would in life. Austen's characters speak in distinctive ways which reveal their personalities. Their speech also varies according to the context. For instance, Mr Bennet's wit has a bitter edge when he is talking to Mrs Bennet: 'You mistake me, my dear. I have a high respect for your nerves' (Vol. 1, Ch. 1, p. 3). When he speaks to Elizabeth, his tone is quite different. When she asks, 'Can [Mr Collins] be a sensible man, sir?' He replies, 'No, my dear; I think not. I have great hopes of finding him quite the reverse.' The key word here is 'hopes' – Mr Bennet trusts Lizzie to understand why he hopes that their guest will be 'a mixture of servility and self-importance' (Vol. 1, Ch. 13, p. 53).

TOP TIP (A02)

Although the structure of Jane Austen's sentences may not be the structure we would usually use today, she regularly read her work aloud to her own family so this remains the best way to catch her elusive, distinctive voice.

TOP TIP (A02)

When writing about the language of a novel you should be ready to consider the following features: voice, dialogue, irony, diction (choice of words), caricature, perspective (point of view) and sentence structure. If this sounds a bit daunting, don't worry. Identifying the technique is Step One but writing about its effect is the more important Step Two. If you can't remember the precise technical term, at least describe how you, as reader, see it working and its effect.

LANGUAGE DEVICE: IRONY

What is irony?	Statements or situations that may suggest something rather different from the obvious meaning.
Example	Elizabeth's hidden anger towards Mr Darcy is revealed in a response to Colonel Fitzwilliam: 'Oh! yes, [...] Mr Darcy is uncommonly kind to Mr Bingley, and takes a prodigious deal of care of him' (Vol. 2, Ch. 10, p. 153).
Effect	The words 'uncommonly' and 'prodigious' are so exaggerated as to suggest she is not sincere.

REVISION FOCUS: AUSTEN'S IRONIC TONE

The narrator's tone is frequently ironic and may also be sarcastic. Read the passage about Lydia's marriage from 'The good news quickly spread' to 'her misery was considered certain' (Vol. 3, Ch. 8, p. 254). Underline some of the words and phrases which suggest that what is said and what is meant are not identical (= irony). Then choose a different colour to underline words that express clear criticism, anger or bitterness and so might better be described as sarcastic or satirical.

LANGUAGE DEVICE: USE OF DETAIL

Pride and Prejudice is full of observations that sum up a whole situation or character in a few words. They often take the form of brief statements, rather than description, and gain their effect through Jane Austen's precise selection of vocabulary (diction) and the strong rhythm of her sentences.

Example	'In as short a time as Mr Collins's long speeches would allow, everything was settled' (Vol. 1, Ch. 22, p. 102).
Effect	The opposites 'short' and 'long' balance each other and offer the reader a quick reminder of just how boring Mr Collins is. It is a measure of the Lucases' relief at Charlotte's engagement that they cheerfully put up with this. If you read the sentence aloud you are likely to find that you stress the word 'everything'. That's it, business concluded, Charlotte's future sorted out – for better or worse.

KEY QUOTATION: THE NARRATOR'S VOICE (A02)

Austen acts in the novel as an **omniscient narrator** (someone who knows about everything). Occasionally she comments on her characters in the first person, for example on Mrs Bennet: 'I wish I could say [that] the establishment of so many of her children, produced so happy an effect as to make her a sensible, amiable, well-informed woman for the rest of her life' (Vol. 3, Ch. 19, p. 319). Putting 'I wish' at the beginning warns the reader in advance that this did not happen.

TOP TIP (A02)

Mrs Bennet characteristically speaks in incomplete sentences – very often with exclamations: 'Every thing that is charming! Three daughters married! Ten thousand a year! Oh Lord!' (Vol. 3, Ch. 17, p. 314) She is illogical and never notices how frequently she changes her mind and contradicts herself.

KEY CONTEXT (A03)

Look out for Austen's use of euphemism (substitution of a less harsh or indirect word or phrase for something embarrassing or unpleasant). The phrase 'secluded in some distant farmhouse' (Vol. 3, Ch. 8, p. 254) means giving birth in secret because unmarried.

LANGUAGE DEVICE: RHETORIC AND SENTENCE STRUCTURES

What is rhetoric?	The skills of using language effectively and persuasively.
Example	Austen and her characters often use rhetorical techniques to make particular points. Lady Catherine tries a rhetorical question: 'Are the shades of Pemberley to be thus polluted?' (Vol. 3, Ch. 14, p. 296) At least she thinks it's a rhetorical question as she assumes the answer must be an obvious 'No'.
Effect	The reader, however, will be guessing (or hoping) 'Yes' and will therefore see Lady Catherine's arrogance more clearly than ever.

Austen uses a wide range of sentence structures for rhetorical effect as well as to illustrate character. Here are some examples:

Example	Effect
A balanced sentence: 'Mr Wickham is blessed with such happy manners as may ensure his *making* friends – whether he may be equally capable of *retaining* them, is less certain.' (Vol. 1, Ch. 18, p. 76)	This makes a true and damning point about Wickham (which Elizabeth ignores). It reveals Darcy's strong character that he can speak in such a controlled manner even when he is clearly upset.
Piling up phrases or **clauses** to make a point more strongly: 'She was a woman of mean understanding, little information, and uncertain temper.' (Vol. 1, Ch. 1, p. 3)	The reader is left in no doubt that the **narrator** dislikes Mrs Bennet.

LANGUAGE DEVICE: DICTION – CONCRETE AND ABSTRACT NOUNS

What are concrete and abstract nouns	**Concrete nouns** are precise and specific names for things. **Abstract nouns** are more likely to be generalised or refer to qualities. Austen uses many more abstract nouns than would be usual today. When she focuses on a specific object it is usually for a special effect.
Example	'Lady Lucas, who had been long yawning at the repetition of delights which she saw no likelihood of sharing, was left to the comforts of cold ham and chicken.' (Vol. 1, Ch. 18, pp. 83–4) 'Delights' and 'comforts' are abstract nouns; 'cold ham and chicken' are concrete and linked to 'comforts' by **alliteration**.
Effect	This gives the impression that Lady Lucas is a straightforward person with rather simple tastes.

TOP TIP A02

Metaphors, similes, imagery, assonance, alliteration, **description** are not frequently used by Austen but they are there in her writing and usually emphasise a particular point. For instance Lady Catherine's accusation that Elizabeth has used 'arts and allurements' (Vol. 3, Ch. 14, p. 293) to capture Darcy is made more powerful by Austen's use of **alliteration**.

TOP TIP A02

If you are asked to comment on a passage, don't rush. Just read carefully, describe the most obvious features you notice and then explain what effect they have on you and what point you think Austen is intending to make. *Pride and Prejudice* wasn't written in a hurry. Austen polished and revised. Remember that whatever is there, is there for a reason.

PROGRESS AND REVISION CHECK

SECTION ONE: CHECK YOUR KNOWLEDGE

1 The three volumes of the novel each have a different main location. Name these locations.

2 Give a practical reason for the novel being divided into three volumes.

3 Volume 1 begins in autumn (Michaelmas) and Elizabeth visits Hunsford in March (Volume 2). Volume 3 begins with Elizabeth and the Gardiners setting out on a holiday. What time of year is it?

4 What is meant by '**voice**'?

5 Give an example of an abstract and a concrete noun from the novel.

6 What is irony?

7 Why would Jane Austen (or her characters) use **rhetoric**?

8 What is an **omniscient narrator**?

9 'Mr Wickham is blessed with such happy manners as may ensure his *making* friends – whether he may be equally capable of *retaining* them, is less certain' (Vol. 1, Ch. 18, p. 76). How would you describe the structure of this sentence?

10 Apart from the narrator, whose is the central perspective on events?

> **TOP TIP** (A01)
>
> Answer these quick questions to test your basic knowledge of the form, structure and language of the novel.

SECTION TWO: CHECK YOUR UNDERSTANDING

Task: Discuss the role that letters play in the structure and **narrative** of *Pride and Prejudice*. Think about:

● How Austen uses letters to move the plot forward
● What we learn about characters through their different voices

> **TOP TIP** (A01)
>
> This task requires more thought and a slightly longer response. Try to write at least three to four paragraphs.

PROGRESS CHECK

GOOD PROGRESS

I can:

● Explain how the writer uses form, structure and language to develop the action, show relationships, and develop ideas. ☐

● Use relevant quotations to support the points I make, and refer to the effect of some language choices. ☐

EXCELLENT PROGRESS

I can:

● Analyse in detail Austen's use of particular forms, structures and language techniques to convey ideas, create characters, and evoke mood or setting. ☐

● Select from a range of evidence, including apt quotations, to infer the effect of particular language choices, and to develop wider interpretations. ☐

UNDERSTANDING THE QUESTION

For your exam, you will be answering a question on the whole text and/or a question on an extract from *Pride and Prejudice*. Check with your teacher to see what sort of question you are doing. Whatever the task, questions in exams will need **decoding**. This means highlighting and understanding the key words so that the answer you write is relevant.

BREAK DOWN THE QUESTION

Pick out the **key words** or phrases. For example:

> **Question:** Read from 'Sir William and Lady Lucas were speedily applied to for their consent' to 'Elizabeth would wonder, and [...] her feelings must be hurt by such a disapprobation.' (Vol. 1, Ch. 22, pp. 102–3)
>
> **How** does Austen **present attitudes** towards **marriage** in **this extract** and in the **novel as a whole**?

What does this tell you?

● Focus on **the theme of marriage** but also on **attitudes** – so give some **different** characters' views on marriage. Does the narrator have a view?

● The word **'present'** tells you to focus on the ways Austen reveals these attitudes. **How** does she do it – **how** does she use language to communicate complex, conflicting ideas and feelings?

● The phrases **'this extract'** and **'novel as a whole'** mean **start** with the given **extract** then **widen your discussion** to the rest of the novel, but stick to the theme **in both**.

PLANNING YOUR ANSWER

It is vital that you generate ideas quickly, and plan your answer efficiently when you sit the exam.

STAGE 1: GENERATE IDEAS QUICKLY

Very briefly **list your key ideas** based on the question you have **decoded**. For example:

In the extract:

● *Charlotte's family give their points of view. Think about these – and narrator's attitude. Is there some criticism implied?*

● *Charlotte reflects on what she has done. Explain her motives.*

In the novel as a whole:

● *Other views of marriage: Mrs Bennet's; Lady Catherine's, etc.*
● *Lydia's marriage – physical attraction*
● *The Gardiners' – a good model*
● *Men and marriage: different motives*

STAGE 2: JOT DOWN USEFUL QUOTATIONS (OR KEY EVENTS)

For example:

From the extract:

● *'Lady Lucas began directly to calculate'* – shows how little her and Mrs Bennet's friendship is worth when there is money at stake – compare Charlotte and Elizabeth?

● *'marriage had always been her object'* – Charlotte is strategic.

● *'Mr Collins [...] was neither sensible nor agreeable; his society was irksome'* – Charlotte knows what she's letting herself in for.

From the novel as a whole:

● *'It is truth universally acknowledged'* – describe the 'neighbourhood view' – as exemplified by the Lucas family and Mrs Bennet. Theme established at start of novel and narrator's attitude

● *'You make me laugh, Charlotte; but it is not sound. You know you would never act in that way yourself'* – an example of narrative irony as well as Elizabeth's good principles and naivety

STAGE 3: PLAN FOR PARAGRAPHS

Use paragraphs to plan your answer. For example:

Paragraph	Point
Paragraph 1:	**Introduce** the **argument** you wish to make: *The importance of marriage as an issue in the novel as shown by the Lucas family reactions, Charlotte's reflections and motives, etc.*
Paragraph 2:	Your first point: *Charlotte's decision has a direct effect on her family (Give examples from extract and analyse language to catch ironic tone)*
Paragraph 3:	Your second point: *Charlotte has already been presented as calculating and strategic in her determination to find a husband (Link back to earlier conversation with Elizabeth about Jane.)*
Paragraph 4:	Your third point: *Marriage involves physical relationship – Charlotte is pregnant by end of novel. Lydia's attraction to Wickham and the Bennets' marriage shows physical attraction not an adequate foundation for happiness.*
Paragraph 5:	Your fourth point: *Elizabeth and Darcy – physical attraction plus suitability and real love – sufficient to make them grow as characters*
Conclusion:	**Sum up** your argument: *Several alternative and not necessarily compatible attitudes to marriage are evident in the extract and the novel as a whole.*

TOP TIP (A02)

When discussing Austen's language, make sure you refer to the techniques she uses, and, most important, the **effect** of those techniques. Don't just say, *Austen uses lots of exclamation marks here.* Write: *Austen's use of exclamation marks shows [or demonstrates or conveys] the ideas that ...*

RESPONDING TO WRITERS' EFFECTS

The two most important assessment objectives are **AO1** and **AO2**.
They are about *what* writers do (the choices they make, and the effects these create), *what* your ideas are (your analysis and interpretation), and *how* you write about them (how well you explain your ideas).

ASSESSMENT OBJECTIVE 1

What does it say?	What does it mean?	Dos and Don'ts
Read, understand and respond to texts. Students should be able to: ● maintain a critical style and develop an informed personal response ● use textual references, including quotations, to support and illustrate interpretations.	You must: ● Use some of the literary terms you have learned (correctly!) ● Write in a professional way (not a sloppy, chatty way) ● Show you have thought for yourself ● Back up your ideas with examples, including quotations	**Don't write:** *Jane is a really nice character. Austen uses lots of nice words to describe her. She's got an 'affectionate heart'.* **Do write:** *Austen presents Jane throughout the novel as a loving, and decent person, for example when she is described as having an 'affectionate heart' in the final chapter. The adjective 'affectionate' signals her kind nature.*

IMPROVING YOUR CRITICAL STYLE

Use a variety of words and phrases to show effects:

Austen suggests ..., conveys ..., implies ..., explores ..., demonstrates ..., signals ..., describes how ..., shows how ....

I/we (as readers) infer ..., recognise ..., understand ..., question ....

For example, look at these two alternative paragraphs by different students about Lady Catherine. Note the difference in the quality of expression:

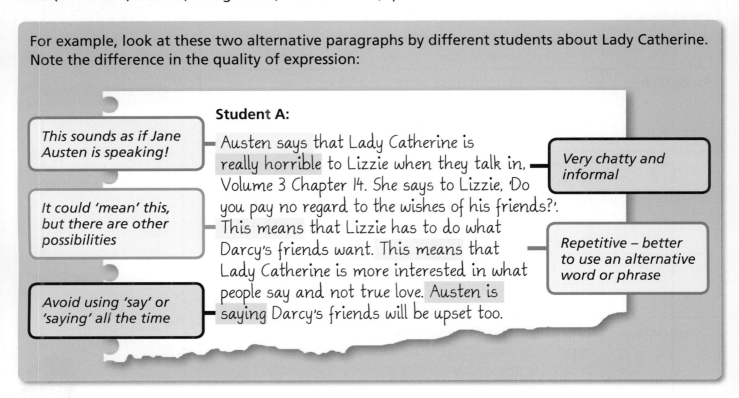

Student A:

This sounds as if Jane Austen is speaking!

It could 'mean' this, but there are other possibilities

Avoid using 'say' or 'saying' all the time

Austen says that Lady Catherine is really horrible to Lizzie when they talk in Volume 3 Chapter 14. She says to Lizzie, 'Do you pay no regard to the wishes of his friends?'. This means that Lizzie has to do what Darcy's friends want. This means that Lady Catherine is more interested in what people say and not true love. Austen is saying Darcy's friends will be upset too.

Very chatty and informal

Repetitive – better to use an alternative word or phrase

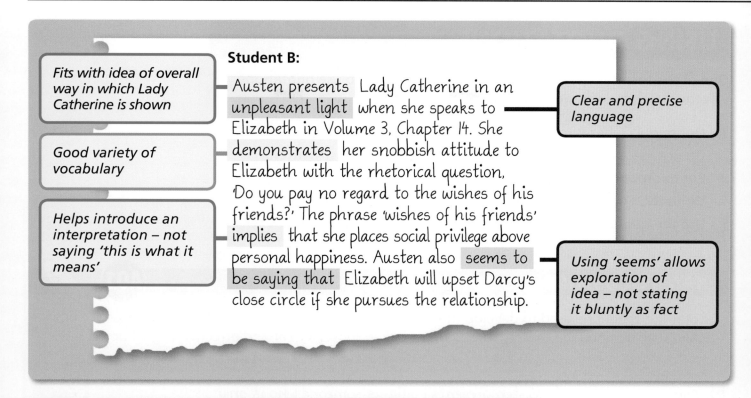

Student B:

Austen presents Lady Catherine in an unpleasant light when she speaks to Elizabeth in Volume 3, Chapter 14. She demonstrates her snobbish attitude to Elizabeth with the rhetorical question, 'Do you pay no regard to the wishes of his friends?' The phrase 'wishes of his friends' implies that she places social privilege above personal happiness. Austen also seems to be saying that Elizabeth will upset Darcy's close circle if she pursues the relationship.

Fits with idea of overall way in which Lady Catherine is shown

Good variety of vocabulary

Helps introduce an interpretation – not saying 'this is what it means'

Clear and precise language

Using 'seems' allows exploration of idea – not stating it bluntly as fact

ASSESSMENT OBJECTIVE 2

What does it say?	What does it mean?	Dos and Don'ts
Analyse the language, form and structure used by the writer to create meanings and effects, using relevant subject terminology where appropriate.	'Analyse' – comment **in detail** on **particular aspects** of the text or language. 'Language' – vocabulary, imagery, variety of sentences, dialogue/speech, etc. 'Form' – how the story is told (e.g. first person narrative, letters, diaries, chapter by chapter?) 'Structure' – the order in which events are revealed, or in which characters appear, or descriptions are presented 'Create meaning' – what can we, as readers, infer from what the writer tells us? What is implied by particular descriptions, or events? 'Subject terminology' – words you should use when writing about novels, such as character, **protagonist, imagery, setting**, etc.	**Don't write:** *The writing is really descriptive in this bit so I get a good picture of Pemberley.* **Do write:** *Austen **conveys** the sense that Pemberley's **setting** impresses Elizabeth as she observes the 'hill, crowned with wood …' which was 'a beautiful object'. The **metaphorical use** of 'crowned' **implies** its, and perhaps Darcy's, majesty.*

THE THREE 'I'S

- The best analysis focuses on specific ideas, events or uses of language and thinks about what is **implied.**
- This means looking beyond the obvious and beginning to draw **inferences.** On the surface, Elizabeth's visit to Pemberley tells us how lovely it is, and how rich Darcy must be, but what deeper ideas does it signify about her relationship to Darcy, or about the way settings are linked to character?
- From the inferences you make across the text as a whole, you can arrive at your own **interpretation** – a sense of the bigger picture, a wider evaluation of a person, relationship or idea.

USING QUOTATIONS

One of the secrets of success in writing exam essays is to use quotations **effectively**. There are five basic principles:

1. Quote only what is most useful.
2. Do not use a quotation that repeats what you have just written.
3. Put quotation marks, e.g. ' ', around the quotation.
4. Write the quotation exactly as it appears in the original.
5. Use the quotation so that it fits neatly into your sentence.

EXAM FOCUS: USING QUOTATIONS A01

Quotations should be used to develop the line of thought in your essay and 'zoom in' on key details, such as language choices. The example below shows a clear and effective way of doing this:

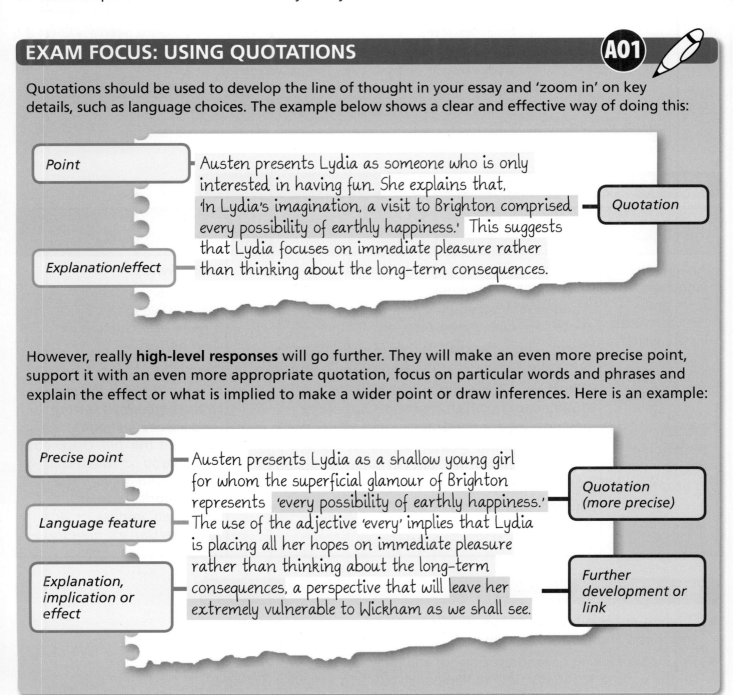

Point — Austen presents Lydia as someone who is only interested in having fun. She explains that, 'In Lydia's imagination, a visit to Brighton comprised — **Quotation** every possibility of earthly happiness.' This suggests that Lydia focuses on immediate pleasure rather **Explanation/effect** — than thinking about the long-term consequences.

However, really **high-level responses** will go further. They will make an even more precise point, support it with an even more appropriate quotation, focus on particular words and phrases and explain the effect or what is implied to make a wider point or draw inferences. Here is an example:

Precise point — Austen presents Lydia as a shallow young girl for whom the superficial glamour of Brighton represents 'every possibility of earthly happiness.' — **Quotation (more precise)** **Language feature** — The use of the adjective 'every' implies that Lydia is placing all her hopes on immediate pleasure rather than thinking about the long-term **Explanation, implication or effect** — consequences, a perspective that will leave her — **Further development or link** extremely vulnerable to Wickham as we shall see.

SPELLING, PUNCTUATION AND GRAMMAR

SPELLING

Remember to spell correctly the **author's** name, the names of all the **characters**, and the **names of places**.

A good idea is to list some of the key spellings you know you sometimes get wrong **before** the exam starts. Then use your list to check as you go along. Sometimes it is easy to make small errors as you write but if you have your key word list nearby you can check spellings.

PUNCTUATION

Remember:

- Use **full stops and commas in sentences accurately to make clear** points. Don't write long, rambling sentences that don't make sense. Equally, avoid using a lot of short repetitive sentences. Write in a fluent way, using linking words and phrases, and use **inverted commas** for **quotations**.

Don't write	Do write
Austen conveys the sense that Pemberley's setting impresses Elizabeth she observes the hill crowned with wood this makes it and Darcy sound majestic.	Austen conveys the sense that Pemberley's setting impresses Elizabeth. She observes the 'hill, crowned with wood' which makes it, and Darcy, sound majestic.

GRAMMAR

When you are writing about the text, make sure you:

- Use the present tense for discussing what the writer does, e.g. *Austen **presents** Elizabeth as an independent young woman* not *Austen **presented** Elizabeth as an independent young woman*.
- Use pronouns and references back to make your writing flow.

Don't write	Do write
Whilst Mr Bennet appeared an intelligent and sensible man, Mr Bennet's lack of control as far as Lydia is concerned made his treatment of Lydia seem foolish.	Whilst Mr Bennet **appears** an intelligent and sensible man, **his** lack of control as far as Lydia is concerned **makes** his treatment of **her** seem foolish.

TOP TIP A04

Remember that spelling, punctuation and grammar are worth **approximately 5%** of your overall marks, which could mean the difference between one grade and another.

TOP TIP A04

Practise your spellings of key literature terms you might use when writing about the text such as: ironic, omnipotent narrator, simile, metaphor, imagery, **protagonist**, character, theme, **hierarchy**, etc.

TOP TIP A04

Enliven your essay by varying the way your sentences begin. For example, *Elizabeth finds herself drawn to Darcy, despite her original misgivings* can also be written as: *Despite her original misgivings, Elizabeth finds herself drawn to Darcy.*

The best way to check that your writing is varied and interesting is to read it back to yourself.

ANNOTATED SAMPLE ANSWERS

This section provides three sample responses, one at **mid** level, one at a **good** level and one at a **very high** level.

> **Question:** Read from: 'Let me be rightly understood' to 'if your nephew does not object to them, they can be nothing to you' (Vol. 3, Ch. 14, pp. 293–5). In this extract Lady Catherine states her objections to Elizabeth marrying Darcy.
>
> How does Austen present the relationship between Lady Catherine and Elizabeth in the novel? Write about:
>
> - How Austen presents Lady Catherine's feelings in this extract
> - How Austen presents the relationship between Lady Catherine and Elizabeth in the novel as a whole

SAMPLE RESPONSE 1

AO1 Introduces basic view of Lady Catherine

Austen presents Lady Catherine as very unpleasant person as she is very nasty indeed to Lizzie in this passage.

AO1 Specific point of view

The way she speaks shows that she thinks she is in charge of the situation. 'Let me be rightly understood' is a very strong statement and makes it sound like a teacher telling off a little child but of course Lizzie is not a child, but a grown woman.

AO1 Quotation but not fluently embedded

AO1 New point clearly signalled in new paragraph

Another thing is that she speaks in a very rude way and says nasty things about Elizabeth. For example, she says, 'of inferior birth, of no importance in the world, and wholly unallied to the family.' By saying she is not important she is making it sound as if Elizabeth is a nobody and that Lady Catherine is like the lady of the manor. This is not a respectful way to talk to anyone let alone someone who is basically a nice person.

AO1 Too informal; needs to have a critical style

AO2 Not relevant to this part of the essay, which is about Lady Catherine

Elizabeth's reply to this is that she says that it doesn't matter if lots of other people wanted Darcy to marry Miss de Bourgh as the most important thing was that he doesn't want to. She says, 'If Mr Darcy is neither by honour nor inclination confined to his cousin, why is not he to make another choice?'

But Lady Catherine won't give up. She is very determined and very unhappy that this young woman is standing up to her. But most important of all she threatens her. 'Your alliance will be a disgrace; your name will never even be mentioned by any of us.'

A02 — Detailed explanation if expressed a bit clumsily

This basically means that if they get married then they not be talked about by any of the rich landowners and the family. So she is saying that they will be embarrassed and shamed by him marrying a common girl. This is not unusual as this is how the rich viewed things in Austen's day.

A03 — Comments on context but could be more developed

To end with she tells Lizzie that she is used to getting her own way which sounds very spoiled and snobbish. This shows that overall she is not a pleasant person at all which is what you see in the rest of the story.

A01 — Attempt to sum up this part of essay but a bit weakly expressed

A01 — Fair point but 'nosy' is too informal for an exam essay

Elizabeth has met Lady Catherine before when she was staying with Charlotte. They didn't get on very well then because Elizabeth didn't want to tell Lady Catherine how old she was and Lady Catherine didn't like not getting an answer. She is used to people flattering her and doing everything she says because she is rich and powerful. Elizabeth just thinks she is nosy. Elizabeth felt all the impertinence of her questions, but answered them very composedly.' That suggests that Elizabeth was trying to be polite.

A02 — Good choice of quotation. Comment could be better focused on words and rhythm of sentence

A02 — Paragraph not sufficiently focused on Elizabeth's relationship with Lady Catherine

Mr Darcy was also staying at Rosings when Elizabeth was there. She expected him to be as snobbish as his aunt and in those days he was. By the time Lady Catherine comes to Longbourn to tell Elizabeth not to marry Darcy, Elizabeth has met him again at Pemberley and she has seen him being polite to her aunt and uncle. So now she can say 'if your nephew does not object to them they can be nothing to you' but she doesn't really know. When Lady Catherine has gone she can't talk to anyone about the conversation because she doesn't know what to think. She knows that she loves Darcy but she doesn't know whether he will listen to his aunt or what Lady Catherine will do next.

MID LEVEL

Comment

There are some good points made here and a viewpoint comes across but the style is rather chatty and informal in places. The writer needs to refer more to Austen herself and what **she** does, and there is little reference to language devices or techniques. There is one comment on context (AO3) but it is very fleeting and generalised.

For a Good Level:

- Use a more formal and critical vocabulary rather than chatty, informal words and phrases.
- Embed quotations into sentences so that they flow and are easy to follow.
- Comment in detail on the effect of language choices made by Austen.
- Stay focused on the question.

SAMPLE RESPONSE 2

A01 Introduction sets up answer well

In this passage, Austen presents Lady Catherine as someone who is snobbish and cruel. It is a really unpleasant conversation between Elizabeth and her, and you really get to see what Lady Catherine is like.

A02 Zooms in on key word and explains its effect

For a start, it seems that Lady Catherine views Darcy almost as her personal property when she says that, 'while in their cradles, we planned the union.' The fact that his marriage was 'planned' even when he was a baby shows how much control she thinks she should have over him. Now she thinks she can control Elizabeth in the same way.

A01 Quotation fluently embedded into sentence

A01 Paragraph introduces new point

A03 Analysis of key word and comment on context

Austen also shows that Lady Catherine has a spiteful, cruel side to her. We can see this when she says that Elizabeth is a young woman of 'inferior birth, of no importance in the world, and wholly unallied to the family!' In those days your family connections were very important. The word 'inferior' tells us that simply because of her family background she is not fit to be Darcy's wife, so not only does she insult Elizabeth but her family too!

Austen also demonstrates this cruel side when Lady Catherine threatens Elizabeth. She says that Elizabeth 'will be censured, slighted, and despised, by everyone connected with him. Your alliance will be a disgrace; your name will never even be mentioned by any of us.' The words 'despised' and 'disgrace' tell us that she thinks the marriage will bring shame on them both and they will be rejected by society and also by friends and family. This is a proper threat as there could be many people, not just Lady Catherine, who would say the marriage 'was unacceptable'.

A01 Clear personal interpretation, well developed

A03 Point taken a stage further in reference to culture of the time

A02 Literary device and its intended effect mentioned but a little bluntly

Austen also shows how Lady Catherine tries to use emotional blackmail. She asks Elizabeth, 'Is this your gratitude for my attentions to you last spring? Is nothing due to me on that score?' These are rhetorical questions. They mean it is 'payback' time for Elizabeth and are meant to make her feel bad and to put her in her place. But they don't because they have the opposite effect as Elizabeth does not feel she owes her anything in any case.

A02

A good point that Elizabeth (and the reader) may have formed an impression of Lady Catherine even before she enters the story

When Elizabeth first encountered Lady Catherine she was staying with Charlotte and Mr Collins and had already heard about Lady Catherine's wealth and grandeur even how much Lady Catherine's husband had spent on his windows! She did not feel intimidated, however, as she had not heard of Lady Catherine possessing any 'extraordinary talents or miraculous virtue'.

During her first evening at Rosings Lady Catherine cross-questioned Elizabeth about herself and her family. Elizabeth felt all the impertinence of her questions, but answered them very composedly.' The word 'impertinence' is quite a surprising one as it suggests Lady Catherine is somehow being rude or cheeky and definitely not behaving as a grand lady should behave. Elizabeth manages to stay calm when she is at Rosings. She can see how Lady Catherine has got used to being flattered and guesses she may be the first person who has ever stood up to her.

A02

Good comment, using a single word to link to the main theme of proper behaviour

A01

Neat link back to the extract. The following paragraph is sound but a little too *narrative* based. It would have been strengthened by one more piece of linguistic analysis

In the extract Elizabeth is still not afraid of Lady Catherine but this time her rudeness and her interference make her angry. She stays calm for as long as she can but eventually she demands to go back to the house. It seems that their relationship is at an end when Lady Catherine says 'I take no leave of you, Miss Bennet' but Jane Austen puts another twist in the story.

GOOD LEVEL

Comment

This is a generally fluent and well-argued response which explores the presentation of Lady Catherine in detail. There is some close analysis of key words and phrases to get points across, and some evidence of personal interpretation. Expression is generally good, and quotations are fluently embedded, but use of words such as 'payback' may be a little too informal.

For a High Level:

- Develop ideas about the social context more fully.
- Expand the style of expression by using a wider vocabulary so more subtle ideas can be developed.
- Vary opening sentences in paragraphs so that the essay can introduce ideas in more interesting ways.

SAMPLE RESPONSE 3

A01 Excellent opening introduction sets up importance of extract in the action of the novel, and in Lady Catherine's presentation

The scene is a defining moment in Austen's telling of the story. The confrontation of Lady Catherine and Elizabeth is like a battle between the old and the new, when selfish arrogance meets true gentility. It represents, in microcosm, the defining themes of the novel, but more specifically, allows us to see Lady Catherine revealed as the arrogant and cruel snob she really is.

A01 Useful reference back to earlier part of novel

Lady Catherine's patronising but ignorant self-importance has already been comically exposed in Elizabeth's visits to Rosings, but here her character is revealed by Austen in all its viciousness. She arrives confident in her demand that Elizabeth should deny any intention of marrying Darcy but when Elizabeth refuses, Austen presents Lady Catherine as resorting to threats, 'You will be censured, slighted and despised'. This pattern of three adjectives is an attempt to hammer home Elizabeth's potential shame.

A02 Clear, detailed analysis supported by well-selected quotation

A02 Excellent development of point, with interpretation of language and effect

Rhetorical language is Lady Catherine's strong point. She likes to hear herself speak and once she has found a certain rhythm or sentence style she finds it hard to stop. Look, for instance, at the sequence of four rhetorical questions beginning 'Do you pay no regard to the wishes of his friends?' They could be real questions if Lady Catherine ever paused for an answer but she does not. She doesn't expect answers, let alone contradictions, so, when Elizabeth does reply, calmly and rationally, Lady Catherine is shocked. 'Now what have you to say?' she asks when she asserts Darcy's engagement to her daughter. Clearly she assumes that Elizabeth will say nothing. However, it is she who has no answer to Elizabeth's logical response. Austen makes silence explicit; 'Lady Catherine hesitated for a moment'.

A02 Good example

A02 Interesting observation on Austen's use of dialogue

During Elizabeth's visits to Rosings there have been plenty of indications that neither logic nor manners are among Lady Catherine's strong points. Even in the minor episode of after-dinner music she has shown her stupidity and conceit. She claims that there are 'few people in England' who have 'more true enjoyment' of music than she does, and she knows she would have been 'a great proficient' - except she has never learned. We, the readers, view Lady Catherine through the narrator's ironic gaze and can assume that Elizabeth also notices that 'Mr Darcy looked a little ashamed of his aunt's ill-breeding.'

A02 Thoughtful insight into narrative voice

A03

Reference to historical period and literary context

'Pride and Prejudice' has links to the eighteenth-century novel of manners and the concept of true gentility is one of its main themes. The example of Lady Catherine shows that there is no inevitable link between gentility and high social class.

Lady Catherine's attempt to bully Elizabeth on her visit to Longbourn is blacker comedy. It comes at a time when Elizabeth is, paradoxically, both more sure of herself and more vulnerable. At Rosings she was able, had she needed to, to place Mr Darcy and his aunt together in the same rich-and-arrogant bracket. Wickham had encouraged this. She could therefore see the ridiculous aspects of Lady Catherine and feel amused, as she had no reason to care for her opinion.

A01

Useful link to earlier in the novel

A01

Good use of 'heroic' – in a romance the hero or heroine has to earn their happy ending

Now the situation is different: Elizabeth knows that she loves Darcy and she also knows that he knows the worst of her family. She does not know what Darcy feels about his aunt or how much he cares about her. Her defiance of Lady Catherine is correspondingly heroic; 'Whatever my connections may be,' says Elizabeth, 'if your nephew does not object to them, they can be nothing to you.' This is a clear and controlled sentence but it still contains uncertainty in the single word 'if'.

Finally, it is structurally brilliant of Austen to make Elizabeth's defiance the catalyst that encourages Darcy to propose again. Lady Catherine prides herself on her 'frankness', which in her case means rudeness, but Darcy knows that for Elizabeth it means honesty. 'Had you been [...] decided against me, you would have acknowledged it to Lady Catherine frankly.' And she replies 'Yes, you know enough of my frankness to believe me capable of that.' Lady Catherine's usefulness can become a joke between them 'and that should make her happy for she loves to be of use.' Her stature has been reduced from bully to go-between.

A01

Good awareness of novel's construction

A01

Excellent synthesis of ideas in final sentence

VERY HIGH LEVEL

Comment

This is an exceptionally fluent answer with an excellent focus on language detail. There is close analysis of key words and phrases to get points across, and clear evidence of personal interpretation and response. Expression is good, and quotations are fluently embedded. A convincingly argued, individual response.

PRACTICE TASK

Write a full-length response to this exam-style question and then use the **Mark scheme** on page 96 to assess your response.

Read from: 'Could Colonel Forster repeat the particulars of Lydia's note to his wife?' to 'Oh! Jane [...] was there a servant belonging to it, who did not know the whole story before the end of the day?' (Vol. 3, Ch. 5, pp. 239–40). In this extract Jane is talking with Elizabeth about Lydia's elopement.

Question: How does Austen present Lydia as naive and thoughtless in the novel?
Write about:

- How Austen presents Lydia in this extract
- How she is presented in the rest of the novel

TOP TIP

You can use the General skills section of the **Mark scheme** on page 96 to remind you of the key criteria you'll need to cover.

Remember:

- Plan quickly and efficiently by using key words from the question
- Focus on the techniques Austen uses and the effect of these on the reader
- Support your ideas with relevant evidence, including quotations

FURTHER QUESTIONS

1. Read from 'Mr Bingley was good-looking and gentlemanlike ...' to 'He was the proudest, most disagreeable man in the world' (Vol. 1, Ch. 3, pp. 6–7). In this extract the local families have come together for a ball at the Assembly Room in Meryton.

   Explore the first impressions of Mr Bingley and Mr Darcy in the extract and consider the relationship of first impressions to the theme of pride and prejudice elsewhere in the novel.

2. *Pride and Prejudice* can be thought of as a romantic comedy. The romance is obvious but where does the comedy lie? Focus your ideas around at least two aspects, e.g. a character, a situation, a language feature.

3. Explore the theme of wealth and property in *Pride and Prejudice*. Think about:

   - The way characters are introduced with reference to their incomes
   - The contrasting ways Lady Catherine and Mr Darcy manage their estates

LITERARY TERMS

abstract noun	something that you cannot experience tangibly (i.e. through your five senses)
alliteration	a series of words with the same first letter or sound, usually consonants
caricature	an exaggerated and simplified description of a character, usually to make them appear comic or ridiculous
character	a person in a piece of writing who has consistent and developed personality traits
clause/subclause	part of a sentence, usually containing a verb
coincidence	an unlikely or unexpected connection between characters or events
concrete noun	something that you can experience, i.e. see, hear, touch, smell or taste
convention	a traditional and generally accepted form; it can apply to social behaviour or ways of presenting plots, characters, situations, etc.
cross-referencing	comparing one part of a text with another
dialogue	a conversation between two or more characters; or the words spoken by characters in general
exclamation	a sharp outcry expressing a strong emotion, often no more than a word or two
foreshadow	act as a warning or sign of something that will occur later
free indirect speech	a method of reporting a character's thoughts and actions as if from their perspective
hero/heroine	the central male/female character, usually admirable. The word **protagonist** also means the central character but is not gender specific
imagery	descriptive language which uses images to make actions, objects and characters more vivid in the reader's mind. Metaphors and similes are examples of imagery.
irony/ironic	a form of words which carries a meaning quite different from what it appears to say. An author or a character within a novel or play may make an ironic statement.
metaphor	a figure of speech in which a word or phrase is applied to an object, character or action which does not literally belong to it, in order to imply a resemblance and create an unusual or striking image in the reader's mind
narrative/narrative perspective	a story, tale or any recital of events, and the manner in which it is told
narrator	the voice telling a story or relating a sequence of events
omniscient narrator	a narrator who uses the third-person narrative ('he', 'she', 'they') and who has access to all the thoughts and feelings of the characters and to events
rhetoric(al)	ways of patterning words to make them more powerful, and/or using language to persuade or convince
sarcasm/sarcastic	an extreme form of irony, usually intended to be hurtful
satire/satirical	a work in which folly, evil or one or more topical issues is held up to scorn through ridicule, irony or exaggeration
simile	a figure of speech which compares two things using the word 'as' or 'like'
style	a writer's distinctive way of using words
theme	a recurring main idea
voice	can be used to refer to the writer's style or to the different ways in which characters speak

CHECKPOINT ANSWERS

CHECKPOINT 1, page 9

Elizabeth visits Kent (Rosings and Hunsford Parsonage) in Volume 1 and Derbyshire (Pemberley and Lambton) in Volume 3.

CHECKPOINT 2, page 13

Mary's piano playing is appreciated when she plays tunes for dancing.

CHECKPOINT 3, page 17

The Bingley sisters are looking forward to the departure of Jane and Elizabeth. They consider the Bennet sisters inferior. Caroline is also becoming jealous of Darcy's interest in Elizabeth.

CHECKPOINT 4, page 18

Mr Collins's hypocrisy is revealed. He lectures the young women on the evils of reading frivolous novels rather than serious sermons before he plays a game of chance. He is totally oblivious to the contradiction.

CHECKPOINT 5, page 19

Elizabeth is so ready to believe Wickham because he reinforces her determination to dislike Darcy and his story seems plausible. Elizabeth is charmed by Wickham and is attracted to him.

CHECKPOINT 6, page 24

Mrs Bennet reacts violently with an outpouring of contradictory thoughts. To see her daughters married is so important that she even blames Elizabeth for ruining the chances of one marriage. She sulks and will not be consoled.

CHECKPOINT 7, page 25

Mr Bennet makes light-hearted fun of Wickham's behaviour, unaware of how dangerous a man he really is. Mr Bennet jokes, but losing the chance of happiness turns out to be a serious matter for both Jane and Elizabeth.

CHECKPOINT 8, page 26

Mrs Gardiner's recollection that she had heard Darcy spoken of as a 'proud ill-natured boy' (Vol. 2, Ch. 3, p. 119) seems to confirm Wickham's story. The memory is very vague, however, and it is only Darcy's father that she clearly remembers. She has never met Darcy.

CHECKPOINT 9, page 27

Elizabeth wants to dislike Darcy, so she appears to enjoy the prospect of him having a 'sickly and cross' wife in Miss de Bourgh. That her thoughts should instinctively turn to Darcy suggests she is more interested in him than she cares to admit.

CHECKPOINT 10, page 28

Darcy has no great affection for his aunt, so his true reason for his visit to Hunsford must be to see Elizabeth. His early arrival suggests how important it is for him.

CHECKPOINT 11, page 35

Lydia announces that Wickham's regiment is moving to Brighton. If Jane and Elizabeth had revealed the truth about Wickham, Mr Bennet might not have allowed Lydia to visit Brighton.

CHECKPOINT 12, page 39

When Elizabeth visits Jane at Netherfield (Vol. 1, Ch. 8, p. 28), Miss Bingley comments to Darcy that Elizabeth's appearance 'looked almost wild'. She tries to link Elizabeth's mud-stained ankles and petticoat to 'an abominable sort of conceited independence'.

CHECKPOINT 13, page 40

Lydia and Wickham would have to reach Gretna Green in Scotland to marry without the proper formalities. Colonel Forster begins to worry about Wickham's intentions when he can trace them only as far as London.

CHECKPOINT 14, page 45

Lady Catherine has set off from Kent to Hertfordshire because she heard 'a report of a most alarming nature'. This was that Jane was 'most advantageously' engaged to Bingley and that Elizabeth might be 'soon afterwards united' to Mr Darcy (Vol. 3, Ch. 14, p. 292). It is never made clear where this second part of the rumour has come from. Ironically it is Lady Catherine's reaction that makes it come true.

CHECKPOINT 15, page 48

The happy ending for Mary Bennet is to be left at home without the competition of her more beautiful sisters.

PROGRESS AND REVISION CHECK ANSWERS

PART TWO, pages 49–50

SECTION ONE

1. Mrs Bennet
2. Mr Bennet
3. Twice
4. Miss Bingley
5. Mr Collins
6. Mr Wickham
7. Lydia yawns violently
8. Mr Collins
9. That she is more interested than she admits
10. That Darcy is keen on Elizabeth
11. Darcy
12. Darcy
13. Three thousand pounds
14. Lydia
15. Brighton
16. Mrs Reynolds, the housekeeper at Pemberley
17. Miss Bingley
18. Letter from Jane
19. Lady Catherine
20. Jane and Bingley, Elizabeth and Darcy

SECTION TWO

Task 1:

- Elizabeth's easy intelligent conversation with Colonel Fitzwilliam about books and music is significant as it alerts Mr Darcy to her social suitability (and possibly her attractiveness to other men).
- The conversation prompts Lady Catherine to interrupt and to make assertions about her own love of music which serve only to reveal her ignorance, conceit and rudeness.
- Mr Darcy walks away from his aunt and stands near the piano when Elizabeth begins to play – as if he is changing his allegiance.
- Elizabeth challenges Darcy 'with an arch smile' (Vol. 2, Ch. 8, p. 144). The subsequent three-way discussion between herself, Darcy and Colonel Fitzwilliam appears to be about social skills (music, dancing, conversation) but is more important as it allows them an opportunity to explore and develop their relationship.

Task 2:

- This is the first time that we have seen Elizabeth challenge her father. She makes it clear that she is worried about the effect of a stay in Brighton on Lydia. Her father's laziness is revealed and later events will show that Elizabeth is right.
- When she speaks of the way Lydia's uncontrolled behaviour reflects on the whole family – 'the very great disadvantage to us all' – (pp. 190–1) it shows that she has learned from her reading of Darcy's letter (Vol. 2, Ch. 13) and has accepted his criticisms. Family is a main theme in the novel and these chapters highlight the parental faults that make the Bennet family flawed.
- The choice of language reveals a subtle change in her relationship with her father. Mr Bennet listens 'attentively' (p. 190) and reassures her 'affectionately' (p. 191). He will not act, however, so she leaves the room feeling 'disappointed and sorry' (p. 192).
- These chapters are also important as they develop the reader's understanding of Lydia's character. As well as her being discussed by her father and sister, we are offered a glimpse into her own imagination where she sees herself 'tenderly flirting with at least six officers at once' (p. 192).

PART THREE, page 63

SECTION ONE

1. Mr and Mrs Philips, Mr and Mrs Gardiner
2. The Bingley sisters (Louisa and Caroline)
3. Lady Catherine is Darcy's aunt and Mr Collins's patron
4. Miss de Bourgh
5. Georgiana Darcy and Lydia Bennet
6. No – he was previously Mayor of Meryton
7. Because she is the plainest of the sisters
8. Mrs Gardiner
9. Mrs Reynolds, the Pemberley housekeeper
10. She is very shy

SECTION TWO

- Lydia is introduced by her mother as 'good-humoured' and described by her father as silly. Austen describes Lydia as having 'high animal spirits' (Vol. 1, Ch. 9, p. 36) but her presentation of Lydia is disapproving and **satirical** rather than affectionate and funny.

- Lydia's complete selfishness and lack of thought for anyone except herself is shown when she meets Jane and Elizabeth at the inn. She speaks 'with perfect unconcern' (Vol. 2, Ch. 16, p. 181), which is a typical phrase. Austen says 'She seldom listened to anybody for more that half a minute and never attended to Mary at all' (p. 184). Her attitude to the waiter in the inn reveals that she hardly sees him as human.

- Lydia is presented satirically in relation to Jane and Elizabeth. For instance when Lydia arrives home as Mrs Wickham, Austen describes Jane as giving Lydia 'the feelings that would have attended herself had she been the culprit' (Vol. 3, Ch. 9, p. 259). This is delicately funny and ironic about Jane but makes Lydia's noisy arrival seem almost brutal: 'Lydia was Lydia still.' She treats Jane with typical insensitivity, demanding her place at the top of the table.

- Lydia and her mother are very alike and Austen presents them both unsympathetically. Her ear for Lydia's speech is so acute that she shows her even dismissing her own mother's affection when Mrs Bennet regrets that she'll live so far away. 'Must it be so?' 'Oh, lord! Yes – there is nothing in that. I shall like it of all things' (Vol. 3, Ch. 9, p. 261).

PART FOUR, page 71

SECTION ONE

1. Marriage and money
2. Mr Bennet must visit Mr Bingley (and Mr Bingley return the visit) before it is proper for Bingley to meet Mr Bennet's family
3. Because England is at war with France
4. The view of Rosings Park
5. The word is Pemberley, the speaker is Lady Catherine de Bourgh
6. Colonel Fitzwilliam
7. A book of sermons
8. Dancing
9. Because the estate is 'entailed' and must go to the closest male relative
10. The position of vicar or rector of a church, with an income and a house included

SECTION TWO

- Caroline and Louisa begin 'abusing' Elizabeth as soon as she is out of the room. Describe their negative language. This is bad manners. The Bingley sisters are revealing themselves not to be as genteel as they pretend.

- They focus on the detail of her dirty petticoat. Generally in the novel the more refined characters do not discuss specific, concrete details. They prefer more abstract language and ideas. Consider Lady Catherine's similar attention to detail. It diminishes her social station.

- Look at the responses of Bingley and Darcy. Bingley shows his kindly, gentlemanlike nature. What does Darcy's response suggest?

- Compare other characters whose manners are either better or worse than their social class might suggest, e.g. Lady Catherine (worse), Mrs Annesley and the Gardiners (better). What does this say about Austen's message about behaviour in the novel as a whole?

PART FIVE, page 77

SECTION ONE

1. Volume 1 – Longbourn (and its neighbourhood), Volume 2 – Rosings (and Hunsford Parsonage), Volume 3 – Pemberley
2. To suit the library market at the time as this was how most people liked to read novels
3. Summer
4. The distinctive tone or style of a character's speech, including the individual tone of the narrator
5. For example: abstract nouns – pride, prejudice; concrete nouns – chicken, petticoat
6. The difference between what is said and what is meant
7. To argue or persuade
8. A story-teller who knows everything that is happening and all the characters' thoughts
9. Balanced
10. The central point of view is Elizabeth's

SECTION TWO

- Mention the large number of letters in the novel. Link with eighteenth-century novels-in-letters (epistolary novels) and also the historical fact that letters were the main means of communication (among those who could write and who could afford the postage).
- Letters which move the plot on – e.g. Jane's letters telling of Lydia's elopement
- Letters that reveal the writer's character – e.g. letters from Mr Collins (important to analyse language and style)
- Mention the reception of letters. Often we learn as much about the character who reads a letter as about the character who wrote it – e.g. Mr Bennet's reception of letters from Mr Collins.

MARK SCHEME

POINTS YOU COULD HAVE MADE

Austen presents Lydia as naive and thoughtless in a variety of ways:

- Repetition of 'laugh(ing)' shows Lydia's inability to take things seriously.
- Her reference to not sending word to Longbourn shows lack of judgement and proper family feeling. Jane reports how badly their parents were affected by the 'joke'.
- Her letter shows Lydia expected Wickham to marry her – 'When I sign my name Lydia Wickham'; seems not to think about money at all.

- Elsewhere in the novel Lydia is presented as loud, brash, physical, well grown (tallest of the sisters), stout; possessing assurance and high animal spirits; interrupting Mr Collins, 'attacks' Bingley, yawning openly when tired
- Mrs Bennet's favourite; shares her mother's indiscriminate love of 'a red coat' and physical attractiveness at same age
- Disgrace to her family, unaware that her behaviour affects anyone else. No capacity to change – untamed, unabashed, wild, noisy, fearless
- Class and manners: not a snob: has no concept of sensitivity or discretion – contrast with Jane and Elizabeth

GENERAL SKILLS

Make a judgement about your level based on the points you made (above) and the skills you showed.

Level	Key elements	Spelling, punctuation and grammar	Tick your level
Very high	**Very well-structured answer which gives a rounded and convincing viewpoint.** You use very detailed analysis of the writer's methods and effects on the reader, using precise references which are fluently woven into what you say. You draw inferences, consider more than one perspective or angle, including the context where relevant, and make interpretations about the text as a whole.	You spell and punctuate with consistent accuracy, and use a very wide range of vocabulary and sentence structures to achieve effective control of meaning.	
Good to high	**A thoughtful, detailed response with well-chosen references.** At the top end, you address all aspects of the task in a clearly expressed way, and examine key aspects in detail. You are beginning to consider implications, explore alternative interpretations or ideas; at the top end, you do this fairly regularly and with some confidence.	You spell and punctuate with considerable accuracy, and use a considerable range of vocabulary and sentence structures to achieve general control of meaning.	
Mid	**A consistent response with clear understanding of the main ideas shown.** You use a range of references to support your ideas and your viewpoint is logical and easy to follow. Some evidence of commenting on writers' effects though more needed.	You spell and punctuate with reasonable accuracy, and use a reasonable range of vocabulary and sentence structures.	
Lower	**Some relevant ideas but an inconsistent and rather simple response in places.** You show you have understood the task and you make some points to support what you say, but the evidence is not always well chosen. Your analysis is a bit basic and you do not comment in much detail on the writer's methods.	Your spelling and punctuation is inconsistent and your vocabulary and sentence structures are both limited. Some of these make your meaning unclear.	